JAMES DOUGLAS

Think Faster with ChatGPT

Mental Shortcuts, Brainstorming Hacks, and Idea Engines

Applebee Press

First published by Applebee Press 2025

First edition

This book was professionally typeset on Reedsy.
Find out more at reedsy.com

Contents

Introduction 1
1 Why You Don't Need to Think Alone Anymore 5
2 How ChatGPT Actually Thinks 11
3 The Prompt Formula for Better, Faster Thinking 19
4 From Foggy Idea to Crystal Clarity 28
5 Thinking in Layers 38
6 Fast Facts, Smarter Questions 48
7 Mental Models on Demand 57
8 Speed Reading for Your Brain 67
9 Decision Sprinting with ChatGPT 77
10 Overcome Mental Blocks Instantly 87
11 The Rapid Ideation Toolkit 96
12 The Problem Solver Protocol 107
13 Reverse Engineer Anything 117
14 Systems That Think for You 126
15 Think in Frameworks 136
16 Reflect, Grow, Repeat 146
17 Learn Anything Faster 155
18 Multiply Your Output 164
19 Build Your Second Brain 173
20 Think Ethically, Use Wisely 182
21 Conclusion: The Future Thinker Is You 189
About the Author 192

Introduction

If you've ever wished you could think faster, write quicker, brainstorm better, or just *get unstuck*—you're in the right place.

Maybe you've stared at a blinking cursor, unsure how to start.

Maybe your ideas feel exciting but scattered.

Or maybe you're simply overwhelmed by how fast the world is moving—and wondering how you're supposed to keep up.

You're not alone.

The truth is, we're all being asked to think, create, and adapt faster than ever before.

But here's the good news:

> *You don't need a bigger brain. You need a better system.*

And now, you have one—powered by AI.

Why This Book, Why Now?

ChatGPT and other AI tools are changing the way we work, learn, and think. What used to take hours—writing emails, brainstorming ideas, researching topics, organizing thoughts—can now be done in minutes.

But most people are still using AI like a search engine or a novelty app.

They're missing the real opportunity.

This book is here to show you how to:

- Ask better questions to unlock better answers
- Build systems that amplify your ideas
- Use AI to boost your clarity, not just your speed
- Create more—without burning out
- Learn faster, reflect deeper, and stay human in the process

This is not a tech manual. It's a thinking playbook.

Think of This as a Brain Upgrade

You already have the raw materials: curiosity, creativity, and drive.

This book adds:

- **Mental shortcuts**: So you can cut through overwhelm and get to clarity faster
- **Brainstorming hacks**: To help you generate better ideas on demand
- **Idea engines**: So you never run out of things to write, say, or solve
- **Real-world prompts**: To help you apply everything immediately

Each chapter is designed to be practical, flexible, and user-friendly—whether you're a writer, entrepreneur, teacher, student, or simply someone who wants to do more with less mental clutter.

You'll get examples, plug-and-play prompts, and strategies that work with the free version of ChatGPT (and even better with GPT-4 or Pro versions).

AI Is Not Replacing You—It's Partnering With You

The fear that AI is coming for your job, your creativity, or your voice is understandable. But it's incomplete.

Yes, AI is powerful. Yes, it's fast.

But no matter how advanced it gets, it still needs something only you can bring:

> *Human insight.*
> *Human intuition.*
> *Human values.*

In other words: **it still needs your brain.**

What this book will help you do is **plug your brain into a more powerful workflow**—one that helps you create, decide, learn, and move forward at the pace you want.

What You'll Be Able to Do by the End

By the final chapter, you'll be able to:

- Use ChatGPT to clarify your thinking and generate better ideas
- Build a personal prompt toolkit for writing, planning, and learning
- Design your own "second brain" to organize thoughts and knowledge
- Multiply your creative output—without sacrificing your voice or values

- Think more clearly and ethically in a fast-moving, AI-augmented world

You'll stop using ChatGPT like a toy—and start using it like a **force multiplier for your mind**.

Let's Start Thinking Faster—Together

You don't need to be tech-savvy.

You don't need to be perfect with prompts.

You just need to be curious—and willing to think in a new way.

This is your invitation to reimagine what your brain can do—with the right support system.

Let's unlock it.

Let's think faster.

1

Why You Don't Need to Think Alone Anymore

Let's start with a confession: for most of our lives, we've been taught that thinking is a solo activity. You sit with a blank page, a quiet room, and a head full of clutter—and you try to sort it out alone. Whether you're brainstorming an idea, solving a problem, or making a big decision, the unspoken rule has always been: *you're on your own*.

But what if that's no longer true?

What if you had a tireless thought partner—one that never gets bored, doesn't interrupt, doesn't judge, and can access a library of human knowledge in milliseconds? That's exactly what you now have with tools like ChatGPT.

This chapter isn't about turning over your brain to artificial intelligence. It's about freeing your brain **to do its best work**—by offloading what slows you down and supercharging what moves you forward.

The Myth of the Lone Genius

The idea of the lone genius is a romantic one. The writer in the cabin. The scientist scribbling equations on a chalkboard. The entrepreneur pacing the floor at midnight, searching for the next big thing.

But it's a myth.

Even the most brilliant minds in history had collaborators, muses, rivals, editors, and sounding boards. Einstein had Grossmann. Mozart had Haydn. Steve Jobs had Steve Wozniak. And now, we have AI.

You're not giving up your originality by thinking with ChatGPT. You're doing what the smartest people have always done: **leveraging collaboration to think better**.

Except now, that collaborator happens to be a machine.

Enter the AI Thought Partner

Think of ChatGPT as your second brain—a fast, flexible, infinitely patient co-thinker that you can access anytime. Need to outline a project? Brainstorm 10 new angles on a problem? Understand a complicated article? Or just get unstuck?

ChatGPT is there.

But—and this is important—it only works well **if you engage with it the right way**. The magic isn't in the AI alone. The magic is in the collaboration between you and it. This is not a vending machine where you pop in a prompt and get a perfect idea. It's more like a conversation with a wise, well-read intern: helpful, capable, and full of insights—but you have to lead.

Let's look at what that partnership can look like in real life.

Real-World Scenarios: How People Are Thinking With ChatGPT

1. The Solo Entrepreneur:

Tina runs a one-woman business selling handmade leather journals. She's overwhelmed by marketing. So she uses ChatGPT to brainstorm Instagram post ideas, draft compelling product descriptions, and even map out her email newsletter sequence. She's still doing the thinking—but now she's doing it with momentum.

2. The College Student:

Miguel is preparing for an oral exam on 20th-century literature. He uses ChatGPT to quiz him, role-play as his professor, and explain difficult literary themes in plain English. It's not cheating—it's accelerated learning. He still studies. He just studies smarter.

3. The Burned-Out Manager:

Darren feels stuck during weekly team meetings. He's supposed to inspire innovation, but his mind is blank. Now, before every meeting, he asks ChatGPT to generate 3 provocative discussion questions based on the team's current goals. The results are practical and surprising—and his team is suddenly more engaged.

None of these people are outsourcing their thinking. They're simply doing it faster, with more support. They're using AI as a mental springboard, not a substitute for their own judgment.

And you can too.

What Thinking With AI Actually Means

Let's get specific. Thinking with AI means using ChatGPT to:

- **Clarify** your own ideas by articulating them in a conversation
- **Generate** multiple options when you're stuck in a binary decision
- **Explore** unfamiliar territory quickly, without getting overwhelmed
- **Reframe** problems from angles you hadn't considered
- **Refine** your rough drafts, outlines, or arguments into something sharper

It's not just about saving time. It's about **expanding what's possible** in the same amount of time. ChatGPT doesn't replace your critical thinking. It accelerates it.

And unlike your own brain, it doesn't forget what you just said. It doesn't need a coffee break. It doesn't care if your idea is weird. It will help you brainstorm 50 names for your project, give you feedback on your elevator pitch, role-play your future customer, and summarize the last five years of industry trends—all in under a minute.

When you treat ChatGPT like a collaborator, not a magic box, you'll start seeing the real power of this tool.

The Thinking Bottleneck (and How AI Solves It)

Why do we get stuck?

Because thinking is messy. We second-guess ourselves. We get overwhelmed by information. We can't always see past our own biases, routines, or mental models.

This is what I call the **thinking bottleneck**—when your brain is capable of more, but your process slows you down. You can feel the weight of ideas pressing against the walls of your mind, but you can't quite squeeze them out.

ChatGPT helps unclog that bottleneck.

It's like having a second mind on demand. One that responds instantly. One that can summarize what you're struggling to express. One that keeps asking, "What about this?"

Even better: it never runs out of ideas.

And when you get into the habit of bouncing thoughts off ChatGPT—asking it to challenge you, support you, or extend your ideas—you begin to build a new kind of muscle: **collaborative cognition**. You're not thinking less. You're thinking better, because you're not thinking alone.

What This Book Will Help You Do

Here's what you'll gain as you move through the chapters ahead:

- A **clear system** for crafting prompts that turn ChatGPT into a real-time brainstorming engine
- Tools to beat analysis paralysis, creative blocks, and decision fatigue
- Frameworks to help you **summarize, prioritize, and clarify** faster than ever before
- Dozens of real-world examples and templates for applying ChatGPT to your work, learning, and creative process
- A mindset shift: from relying solely on your own brainpower to **leveraging AI as a creative amplifier**

You'll learn how to use ChatGPT to write, decide, plan, explore, study, design, debate, refine, and think with greater clarity and velocity.

And it all starts with asking better questions—and giving yourself permission to collaborate with the machine.

One Last Thing Before We Dive In

Don't worry if you're not tech-savvy. You don't need to "speak code" to get the most out of this book—or this technology.

If you can have a conversation, you can use ChatGPT.

If you can explain your idea out loud, you can build it faster with AI.

If you've ever written a to-do list, sent an email, or Googled something in a panic, you already know more than enough to get started.

This book will simply give you the tools and tactics to think faster, more clearly, and more creatively—with AI as your thought partner, not your replacement.

Ready?

Let's move from overwhelm to opportunity.

Let's stop thinking alone.

2

How ChatGPT Actually Thinks

Let's clear something up right away: **ChatGPT isn't human, and it doesn't think like one.**

It doesn't dream. It doesn't feel. It doesn't truly "understand" the way we do.

But—and this is important—it *mimics* human thinking in a way that's useful, consistent, and sometimes shockingly insightful.

To use ChatGPT well, you don't need to become an AI expert.

But you do need to understand one thing: **how it thinks *differently* than you do.**

This chapter is your user's guide to the AI brain—not a technical manual, but a peek under the hood. We'll explore how ChatGPT processes language, what it's good (and bad) at, and how you can "think with it" more effectively.

ChatGPT Isn't Smart. It's Trained to Sound Smart.

ChatGPT is a **language model**—not a logic machine, not a fact engine, not a sentient robot. It was trained on an enormous amount of text data: books, articles, websites, conversations, and more. From that training, it learned the patterns of language. Not truths. Not emotions. **Patterns.**

It works by predicting the most likely next word, one token at a time, based on the context of what you've written.

When you type, "Tell me five ways to improve my focus," ChatGPT doesn't consult a neuroscience textbook. It searches through its learned patterns and assembles a response that **sounds** like something a helpful, intelligent person might say based on millions of examples.

This means it's **incredibly good at forming sentences, ideas, outlines, and responses** that feel human. But it also means:

- It sometimes makes things up (this is called **hallucination**).
- It can sound confident while being wrong.
- It doesn't actually know what's *true*—only what's *likely* based on patterns.

So how does this help us?

It means ChatGPT is an excellent **co-thinker**—an idea expander, a wordsmith, a pattern matcher. You feed it the right inputs, and it helps you get unstuck, gain momentum, or see something in a new way.

But to do that, we have to respect how it "thinks."

Think of ChatGPT Like a Super-Fast Improv Actor

Imagine a brilliant improvisational actor who can take on any role—teacher, coach, historian, poet, startup advisor—and improvise convincingly in seconds. Now imagine that actor is mute until you give them direction. That's ChatGPT.

It's not reading your mind. It's responding to your prompts.

If your question is vague, the answer will be vague. If your question is specific, the answer gets sharper. If you build a conversation with context—feeding it your goals, your tone, your perspective—you'll get much better responses.

In other words: **you don't need to know how ChatGPT works behind the scenes. You need to know how to *work with it*.**

Here's how.

The Three Big Ideas That Will Change How You Use ChatGPT

1. **It Thinks in Probabilities, Not Beliefs**

Humans think with intuition, emotion, memory, and logic. ChatGPT doesn't. It builds each response based on the most statistically likely next word—*not* the "best" or "most accurate" word, just the one that most often follows the pattern you've given it.

This is why you can get multiple, different answers to the same question. It's not confused—it's probabilistic. This variability is powerful for creativity and brainstorming, but it also means:

> ***You are responsible for evaluating the answers.***

Don't treat AI output as gospel. Treat it as a springboard.

2. **It Responds Better to Role-Playing and Framing**
If you say:

> *"Explain quantum computing."*
> *You'll get a generic explanation.*

But if you say:

> *"Act like a college professor explaining quantum computing to a high school student using simple metaphors," you'll get something far more helpful—and readable.*

That's because ChatGPT takes your instructions seriously. The more **role**, **tone**, and **context** you provide, the better it can simulate the kind of thinking you want.

Think of it as loading the software with a temporary personality.

3. **It Can Remember in Short Bursts (but Not Long-Term)**
In a single session, ChatGPT can remember what you've said earlier in the conversation. It keeps a rolling memory of recent context—what you're working on, what you've asked for, what examples you gave. But it doesn't retain information from one session to the next unless you're using advanced features like custom instructions or memory (available in some versions).

So if you're having a long, complex conversation—say, about writing a book—you might need to remind it of key ideas along the way.

> *Tip:* ***Summarize your goal every few steps.*** *This helps the AI stay on track and think "with" you instead of drifting.*

Why This Matters to Your Thinking Process

Let's step back for a moment.

You now know:

- ChatGPT doesn't *know* things; it predicts what fits.
- It doesn't make judgments; it mirrors your prompts.
- It doesn't care about truth or falsehood; it cares about linguistic patterns.

So why is it so useful?

Because human thinking isn't perfect either. We forget things. We jump to conclusions. We get emotionally biased. And we often lack the time or mental energy to explore ideas from multiple perspectives.

That's where ChatGPT shines:

- It can help you **rephrase your thoughts** for clarity.
- It can generate **opposing viewpoints** to challenge your assumptions.
- It can offer **analogies, summaries, and reframes** that unlock new insight.
- It can process a page of text faster than you can finish your coffee.

It's not thinking for you—it's **expanding the space around your thinking.**

Avoiding Common Misunderstandings

Because ChatGPT feels human in conversation, it's easy to over-trust or under-use it. Here are a few pitfalls to avoid:

Expecting Perfection

Don't ask for "the best marketing plan" and expect brilliance in one shot. It's better to start with:

> *"Give me 3 rough marketing ideas for a wellness brand targeting busy moms."*

Then iterate.

Blaming the Tool for a Bad Prompt

A generic prompt leads to a generic answer. Add detail. Add structure. Add purpose. You'll be amazed at how much better the output gets.

Thinking You're Cheating

Using ChatGPT to brainstorm, summarize, or think through options is no more "cheating" than using a calculator in a math class. It's a tool. How you use it determines the ethics.

Putting It All Together

Let's recap with a metaphor:

ChatGPT is a mirror made of words.

It reflects your questions, your tone, your structure—and gives it back in a form you can build on.

If you give it garbage, it polishes it.

If you give it clarity, it amplifies it.

If you give it curiosity, it multiplies it.

When you understand how ChatGPT "thinks"—with patterns,

probabilities, and prediction—you stop treating it like a magic 8-ball and start treating it like what it really is:

a co-thinker with no ego, no exhaustion, and endless potential.

Try This: Mini Challenge

Open ChatGPT and try each of the following:

1. Ask a vague question: "How do I improve my focus?"
2. Then ask it again with framing:

   "Act like a peak performance coach helping a busy executive who works remotely. Suggest 5 science-backed strategies to improve focus during work hours."

1. Feed it a messy paragraph from your writing or thinking and ask:

   "Can you rephrase this to sound clearer and more persuasive for a general audience?"

1. Say:

   "Play devil's advocate. What's the downside of the idea I just shared?"

Notice the difference?

This is collaborative thinking in action.

In the next chapter, we'll take this to the next level. You'll learn a simple **Prompt Formula** that makes your thinking with ChatGPT more productive, creative, and lightning-fast—whether you're brainstorming, problem-solving, or just trying to clarify your next move.

Ready to level up?

Let's go.

3

The Prompt Formula for Better, Faster Thinking

By now, you understand that ChatGPT is a thinking partner that works based on how you engage with it. But here's the key insight of this chapter:

> ***The quality of your results depends on the quality of your prompts.***

A prompt is more than just a question. It's a tool. A strategy. A **conversation starter that shapes the direction, tone, and usefulness** of the AI's response.

Think of prompting like driving. If you say, "Take me somewhere," you might end up in a ditch. But if you say, "Take me to the best taco spot within 15 miles that's open past 9 p.m.," now you're going somewhere specific—and satisfying.

In this chapter, I'll give you a simple, repeatable formula to help you craft effective prompts that sharpen your thinking and make ChatGPT your smartest ally.

The Fast Thinker's Prompt Formula

Here's the formula you'll come back to again and again:

R + A + T + C

- **R = Role**: Who should ChatGPT pretend to be?
- **A = Action**: What do you want it to do?
- **T = Topic**: What subject, idea, or challenge are you working on?
- **C = Context**: What background or details will help it respond better?

Let's break this down with examples and use cases.

R = Role

One of the most underused—but most powerful—prompting tools is assigning a **role**.

Instead of asking ChatGPT as a blank-slate assistant, tell it who to *act* like. When you set a role, you shape the perspective, tone, and expertise it brings to the conversation.

Here are a few examples:

- "Act like a productivity coach..."
- "Take on the role of a marketing strategist at a startup..."
- "Pretend you're a college professor explaining this to a high schooler..."
- "You are a creative writing teacher helping a student with writer's block..."

Pro Tip: *The more specific the role, the more useful the*

> *results.*

Compare this:

> *"Give me feedback on this sentence."*

To this:

> *"Act like an experienced editor at a publishing house. Give me constructive feedback on this sentence to improve clarity and flow."*

The second one will get you better results—every time.

A = Action

Now that you've assigned a role, tell ChatGPT **what to do**.

This is your verb. Are you asking it to brainstorm? Summarize? Critique? Explain? Create?

Here are a few action words that work well:

- brainstorm
- summarize
- compare
- rewrite
- critique
- outline
- simplify
- translate
- suggest
- role-play

Choose just one action at a time for clarity. Think of it like giving instructions to a helpful intern: simple, specific, and direct.

> ***Examples:***
> *"Summarize this..."*
> *"Brainstorm five names for..."*
> *"Outline the pros and cons of..."*
> *"Explain this concept as if I'm new to the topic..."*

T = Topic

This is the *what* of your prompt.

Be as specific as you can with the subject you want to explore. If the topic is too broad, the answer will be shallow or scattered.

Example:

- Weak: "Write something about creativity."
- Strong: "Write a short paragraph explaining why constraints can boost creativity in artists."

Think like a teacher writing a test question: **What topic are you focusing on, and what angle do you want to explore?**

> ***Another example:***
> *"You're a startup mentor (Role). Brainstorm (Action) three new customer acquisition strategies (Topic) for a subscription-based fitness app (Context)."*

Now we're getting somewhere.

C = Context

This is what most people skip—but it makes all the difference.

Context gives ChatGPT **what it needs to tailor the response to your situation**. This might include:

- Your audience
- The tone or style you want
- Constraints (word count, format, timeframe)
- Background info (who you are, what you're working on, what the goal is)

> ***Without context:***
> *"Write a blog intro about time management."*
> ***With context:***
> *"Act as a business coach. Write a 3-sentence blog intro on time management for busy solopreneurs who struggle with procrastination. Make it sound motivational and personal."*

Big difference.

Why This Formula Works

The R+A+T+C formula works because it helps ChatGPT "think" the way you want it to. You're guiding the AI through the same mental process a skilled human would go through:

- Adopting a perspective (Role)
- Focusing on the task (Action)
- Targeting a subject (Topic)

- Understanding the situation (Context)

With this formula, you're **not just asking questions—you're shaping results**.

Real-World Prompt Examples

Here are a few complete prompts using the formula:

1. Creative Brainstorming

   Prompt:
   "You're a bestselling author and creativity coach. Brainstorm five story ideas based on the theme 'second chances' that would appeal to readers of contemporary romance. Keep each idea under 50 words."

2. Decision Making

   Prompt:
   "Act as a career advisor. Compare the pros and cons of taking a remote job with flexible hours vs. a local office job with higher pay. Assume I'm a parent of two young kids looking for work-life balance."

3. Studying and Learning

   Prompt:
   "You're a physics tutor for high school students. Explain Newton's three laws of motion in plain language using real-life examples, and make it engaging for a 16-year-old."

4. Planning

> ***Prompt:***
> *"Act like a productivity expert. Create a one-week morning routine plan for a freelance writer struggling with motivation and late-night habits. Make sure each day includes a habit-building activity and a small creative task."*

Troubleshooting Prompts: When the AI Misses the Mark

Even with the best prompts, sometimes ChatGPT gives answers that are:

- Too vague
- Too long
- Too robotic
- Missing the point

Here's what you can do:

Refine, Don't Rewrite

Instead of starting over, say:

> *"That's not quite what I was looking for. Can you simplify that?"*
> *"Add more emotion to this response."*
> *"Can you give me shorter bullet points instead of a long paragraph?"*

ChatGPT loves feedback. Treat it like a real-time editor that can instantly revise and reshape.

Iterate With Follow-Ups

Think of your prompt as the *first draft of a conversation.* Use follow-ups to narrow the focus.

Try:

- "Give me more examples."
- "What's an unconventional way to approach this?"
- "What would a skeptic say about this idea?"

Each question pulls the thinking deeper.

Quick Prompt Builder Exercise

Let's build a prompt together using the R+A+T+C method.

GOAL: You want ideas for a new online course.

- **R (Role):** "Act as a digital education strategist."
- **A (Action):** "Brainstorm"
- **T (Topic):** "topics for a short online course"
- **C (Context):** "The course should appeal to stay-at-home parents who want to earn side income using skills they already have. Keep the ideas practical and low-cost."

> ***Final Prompt:***
>
> *"Act as a digital education strategist. Brainstorm five online course topics that would appeal to stay-at-home parents who want to earn side income using skills they*

already have. Keep the ideas practical, low-cost, and beginner-friendly."

You just built a high-leverage prompt—and gave the AI what it needs to think like a collaborator.

Recap: The Prompt Formula

Remember this:

> ***R + A + T + C***
> *Role + Action + Topic + Context = Better Thinking with ChatGPT*

Whether you're clarifying a problem, exploring an idea, or planning your next creative move, this formula helps ChatGPT become more than a chatbot—it becomes a **thinking engine that responds to your direction.**

You're not just saving time. You're upgrading your brain.

In the next chapter, we'll take this further and explore how to move from vague ideas to **crystal clarity** using ChatGPT—perfect for when you're stuck, scattered, or staring at a blank page.

Let's keep thinking faster.

4

From Foggy Idea to Crystal Clarity

You know that feeling when you have an idea—but it's still fuzzy around the edges?

You can't quite explain it, but you can *feel* that it's good. It's there, somewhere in your head, like a foggy figure waiting to emerge. You just need help pulling it into the light.

That's what this chapter is about.

Even the smartest people struggle to take an unshaped idea and turn it into something clear, structured, and usable. We get stuck in our heads, paralyzed by the gap between what we *mean* and what we *say*.

But when you have a tool like ChatGPT, you don't have to stay stuck. You can take that blurry thought and run it through a process that brings definition, depth, and direction—fast.

Let's walk through how to do exactly that.

Why Our Ideas Start Out Foggy

Before we talk solutions, let's talk reality: **human thinking is naturally messy.**

We often:

- Jump from idea to idea without finishing a thought
- Struggle to explain things clearly, even to ourselves
- Forget what we're trying to say halfway through saying it
- Feel overwhelmed by all the possible directions a single idea could go

This isn't a flaw—it's just how minds work. We're not computers. We're creators. But creators often need a tool to help **organize** the raw material of their minds into something actionable.

That's where ChatGPT shines.

When used with intention, it becomes a kind of **mental mirror**—reflecting your thoughts back in a way that's clearer, tighter, and more structured than when you started.

Step 1: Say It Messy, Say It Anyway

The first rule of thinking with ChatGPT?

> ***Start before you're ready.***

You don't need to write a perfect prompt. You don't even need a full sentence. You just need to get your *messy*, *half-formed*, *rambling* idea out of your head and into the conversation.

Here's what that might look like:

> *"I'm trying to figure out how to explain this idea about how people spend too much time optimizing their productivity systems instead of actually doing the work... I want to write about that but I'm not sure where to start."*

That's not polished. It's not even structured. But it's enough.

ChatGPT might respond:

> *"That's an interesting concept. You could approach it by discussing the difference between productivity* tools *and productivity* results. *Would you like help outlining this as a blog post or identifying key points?"*

Now we're moving.

This step is all about **momentum over mastery**. ChatGPT won't judge your grammar, your typos, or your lack of direction. That's the beauty of it. It meets you wherever you are—and starts helping.

Step 2: Ask for Clarification Help

Once you've spilled your raw thoughts, the next step is to say:

> *"Help me clarify this."*

Or:

- "Can you help me rephrase that more clearly?"
- "What's the main point I'm trying to make here?"
- "How would you turn this into a sentence someone else would understand?"

Now ChatGPT becomes your clarity coach. It can:

- Pull out key themes
- Distill your messy paragraphs into one clean line
- Reorganize scattered thoughts into bullet points
- Ask *you* questions that help you figure out what you really mean

Example:
You say:

> *"I'm thinking about launching a service where I help small businesses with their online presence—like websites, social media, branding—but I don't know what to call it or how to describe it."*

ChatGPT might reply:

> *"Sounds like you're offering digital presence consulting for small businesses. Would you like help crafting a short pitch that describes your service clearly in one sentence?"*

Boom. That fuzzy idea just got a name. And now it's on its way to becoming real.

Step 3: Break It Into Pieces

Big ideas are hard to tackle all at once. That's why one of the best uses of ChatGPT is to say:

> *"Break this down for me."*

You can even prompt it like this:

- "Turn this idea into 3 key points."
- "Can you split this into sections for a blog post?"
- "Help me outline this step-by-step."

When you chunk your thinking, you go from "I don't know where to start" to "Oh, now I have a structure."

Let's say you tell ChatGPT:

> *"I want to write about why failure is underrated and how people can reframe it as a learning tool."*

Now prompt:

> *"Help me break this into a 3-part blog post outline."*

ChatGPT replies:

1. **Why We Avoid Failure** – Social pressure, fear, perfectionism
2. **What Failure Actually Teaches Us** – Resilience, clarity, course correction
3. **How to Reframe Failure in Real Life** – Personal stories, mental shifts, practical exercises

Now your foggy idea has a skeleton. And you didn't have to create it from scratch.

Step 4: Rephrase for Power and Precision

Sometimes you know what you want to say—but not how to say it.

That's when you ask ChatGPT to rephrase.

Try:

- "Rewrite this to sound more confident."
- "Can you make this sound more persuasive?"
- "I want this paragraph to hit harder. Help me punch it up."

This is especially useful when:

- Writing headlines or titles
- Crafting elevator pitches
- Drafting bios, product descriptions, or social posts

Example:

You write:

> *"I help people figure out what they want to do in life and how to stop procrastinating."*

ChatGPT version:

> *"I help ambitious people overcome procrastination and get clear on their life's direction—so they can take meaningful action, faster."*

Small change. Big difference.

Rephrasing helps you find your voice *faster* by showing you what's possible. You can always revise the AI's suggestion, but it gives you a place to start.

Step 5: Ask, "What Am I Missing?"

Once your idea starts to take shape, use ChatGPT as a critical thinking partner. Say:

> *"What am I not seeing?"*
> *"What's a potential counterargument?"*
> *"Are there any gaps in this idea?"*
> *"How would someone from a different industry view this?"*

This is how you turn a *clear* idea into a *strong* idea.

By exploring alternate perspectives, you avoid blind spots and sharpen your thinking.

Example Prompt:

> *"I'm writing a piece arguing that AI won't replace creativity—it will enhance it. Can you list 3 potential counterpoints someone might make, so I can address them?"*

ChatGPT might respond:

1. AI-generated content may reduce demand for human artists
2. Creativity could be commodified or automated
3. People may rely on AI too heavily, weakening original thought

Now you've got direction—and you can use these points to make your argument stronger and more nuanced.

From Idea to Clarity: A Sample Walkthrough

Let's say you start with this:

> *"I kind of want to do something that combines coaching, creativity, and mental health—but I don't know how to frame it."*

Watch the transformation:

1. **Say it messy**
2. You input that raw thought into ChatGPT.
3. **Ask for clarification**
4. You prompt:

> *"Can you help me clarify what I'm trying to say in one sentence?"*

1. **Break it down**

> *"Can you outline 3 ways someone might offer a service like this?"*

1. **Rephrase and refine**

> *"Now rewrite that in a warm, inspiring tone as a tagline."*

1. **Challenge it**

> *"What would someone skeptical of this offering say? How could I address that?"*

By the end of this process, you have:

- A one-line elevator pitch
- A clear outline of your service
- A tagline that resonates
- A stronger, more defensible concept

All from one vague, foggy idea.

The Clarity Cycle

When in doubt, return to this 5-step cycle:

1. **Start messy**
2. **Clarify the core idea**
3. **Break it into parts**
4. **Rephrase with style**
5. **Challenge and refine**

This is how you **turn confusion into clarity**—over and over again.

And once you do, you'll stop wasting energy trying to "figure it all out" in your head. You'll get it *out*, shape it *with* AI, and move *forward* with confidence.

Think Faster, Clearer, Braver

Clarity isn't just about writing clearly. It's about thinking clearly. When your ideas are organized, you act faster. You speak with more conviction. You build with more energy.

ChatGPT isn't just a productivity tool—it's a **thought accelerant**. And when you use it to organize your ideas, simplify your message, and test your assumptions, you become a better thinker.

Fog is part of the process. But now, you don't have to stay there long.

Let's move from fuzzy to focused. From abstract to actionable.

In the next chapter, we'll explore how to **think in layers**—a powerful approach to prompting that helps you zoom in and out of a topic with clarity and precision.

Let's keep thinking faster.

5

Thinking in Layers

Every idea, problem, or plan has layers.

There's the **big-picture overview**, the **core components**, the **fine details**, and then the **real-world application**. The best thinkers—whether strategists, designers, writers, or entrepreneurs—learn how to move fluently between these layers, zooming in to deepen their insight and zooming out to regain perspective.

This mental agility is powerful, but it's also exhausting—especially when you're trying to juggle everything in your head.

That's where ChatGPT becomes your secret weapon. When prompted the right way, it can act like a dynamic lens for your thinking. You can use it to:

- Zoom out for high-level summaries
- Zoom in for details
- Explore middle layers for structure and flow
- Bridge abstract concepts to tangible actions

In this chapter, you'll learn how to use **layered thinking** with

ChatGPT to better understand your ideas, map them more clearly, and communicate them with power.

Why Layered Thinking Works

Let's take a simple example: **planning a book**.

The top layer is your big idea—maybe it's a book about overcoming creative burnout.

The next layer might be a rough structure—say, a three-part model: burnout, recovery, reinvention.

The layer beneath that includes the individual chapters, core arguments, and examples.

And beneath *that* are subpoints, exercises, case studies, and stories.

Most people get lost trying to think across all these layers at once.

Layered thinking helps you slow down, sort ideas by depth, and then build upward or downward as needed.

When you apply this method using ChatGPT, you're no longer alone in organizing your thoughts. You can literally say:

- "Give me a high-level summary."
- "Expand this section with examples."
- "What are the key components?"
- "How would you explain this to a beginner?"
- "Now translate this into action steps."

It's like having a mental elevator: you choose the floor, and ChatGPT meets you there.

The Four Core Layers of Thought

Here's a simple model to remember:

1. Overview (Top Layer)

This is the bird's-eye view. The 30,000-foot summary. It answers:

- What's the big idea here?
- Why does it matter?
- What's the point?

2. Structure (Middle Layer)

This is the skeleton. The outline. It answers:

- What are the key components?
- How does this idea break down logically?
- What are the parts and how do they fit together?

3. Depth (Detail Layer)

This is the substance. The arguments. The content. It answers:

- What's the evidence or reasoning?
- What are the stories, examples, or stats?
- What's happening within each part?

4. Action (Application Layer)

This is the real-world stuff. It answers:

- What do I do with this?
- How do I apply it?
- What's the next step?

Each layer supports the one above it. And when you learn to navigate up and down, you become a more flexible and powerful thinker.

ChatGPT in Layer Mode: How to Prompt for Each Level

Here are sample prompts for each layer. Try them with *any* topic you're exploring:

Layer 1: Overview Prompts

- "Summarize this idea in one sentence."
- "Give me a one-paragraph explanation of [topic] for someone who's never heard of it."
- "What's the core argument here?"
- "What's the 'big picture' of this concept?"

Example:

> *"Summarize the concept of 'emotional intelligence' in 50 words or less."*

Layer 2: Structure Prompts

- "Break this down into 3 main components."
- "What are the essential parts of this framework?"
- "Can you outline this as a blog post/book/video script?"
- "Map the structure of this argument."

Example:

> *"Break the idea of 'deep work' into its key principles and organize them into a logical sequence."*

Layer 3: Depth Prompts

- "Expand this section with examples and explanations."
- "Add more depth to this argument."
- "Give me 3 supporting stories, quotes, or case studies."
- "What research or data backs this up?"

Example:

> *"Expand on the idea that multitasking reduces productivity with examples from science or real life."*

Layer 4: Application Prompts

- "Turn this idea into a checklist or action plan."
- "How can someone apply this in their daily routine?"
- "What are the first 3 steps someone should take?"
- "Give me practical use cases for this concept."

Example:

> *"Turn the idea of 'mindful communication' into a 5-step guide for teams."*

Layered Thinking in Action: A Case Study

Let's walk through a real example—say, you want to write about the concept of **"digital minimalism."**

Step 1: Ask for an overview

> *"Give me a one-paragraph summary of digital minimalism."*

ChatGPT replies:

> *"Digital minimalism is a lifestyle philosophy that encourages intentional and limited use of digital tools to focus on what truly matters. It involves reducing online distractions, setting boundaries with technology, and reclaiming time and attention for more meaningful activities."*

Step 2: Ask for structure

> *"Break this idea into 3 main parts for a blog post."*

ChatGPT replies:

1. **Recognizing Digital Clutter**

2. **Setting Boundaries and Rules**
3. **Reclaiming Focus and Purpose**

Step 3: Ask for depth

> *"Expand point 2 with real-life examples and specific suggestions."*

ChatGPT replies:

> *"Point 2 involves creating rules for tech use, such as scheduling social media time, disabling non-essential notifications, or implementing 'no-screen' zones at home. For instance, someone might decide to only check email twice a day or delete apps that don't align with their goals."*

Step 4: Ask for application

> *"Turn this into a 7-day digital detox plan."*

ChatGPT responds with:

- **Day 1:** Audit your screen time
- **Day 2:** Remove low-value apps
- **Day 3:** Set notification preferences
- ... and so on

Suddenly, you've gone from an abstract concept to a clear, structured, detailed, and actionable project.

This is layered thinking—powered by prompts.

Layer Ladder: A Prompt Template You Can Use Anywhere

Here's a reusable template for working through any idea, step-by-step:

1. **"What's the big idea here?"** (overview)
2. **"Break it into parts."** (structure)
3. **"Go deeper on this section."** (depth)
4. **"What can someone *do* with this?"** (application)

Use this any time you're feeling stuck. It works for:

- Outlining a podcast episode
- Writing an essay
- Preparing a talk
- Planning a business offer
- Creating an online course
- Studying a new concept

It's like a mental Swiss Army knife—and ChatGPT is your guide through every layer.

Zoom In. Zoom Out. Repeat.

One of the most powerful habits you can build is the ability to:

- Zoom **out** to gain clarity and direction
- Zoom **in** to fill in gaps and add richness
- Zoom **out again** to check alignment
- Zoom **in again** to refine details
- And finally, zoom **forward** into action

Using ChatGPT for this process means you don't have to hold everything in your brain. You can treat it like a thinking journal—one that summarizes, organizes, and expands your ideas in real time.

Bonus Use: Ask for Layered Explanations

Let's say you're learning a new concept—like blockchain.
You can tell ChatGPT:

> *"Explain blockchain to me in three layers:*

1. Like I'm 5 years old
2. Like I'm a college student
3. Like I'm an expert building an app on it"

This not only teaches you—it trains *you* to think in layers.

Recap: Layered Thinking = Mental Clarity on Demand

Let's review the key takeaways:

- Every idea has multiple layers: overview, structure, depth, and application
- ChatGPT can help you navigate these layers with specific prompts
- Thinking in layers improves clarity, communication, and action
- You can build outlines, expand content, simplify complexity, and spark insight—fast
- Use the **Layer Ladder** template to break down *any* idea into

usable parts

You don't have to keep every layer of a project or concept in your head anymore. With ChatGPT, you can move between levels of thinking without losing your thread.

Now you're not just thinking faster. You're thinking smarter.

In the next chapter, we'll explore how to **use ChatGPT for rapid research and smarter questions**—so you can make faster, better-informed decisions without getting buried in information overload.

Let's keep going. The next level of thinking starts now.

6

Fast Facts, Smarter Questions

Information is everywhere—but insight is rare.

We live in an age where you can Google anything, but that doesn't mean you understand it. We scroll through endless content, bookmark articles we'll never read, and spend hours "researching" only to end up more confused than when we started.

That's not your fault. The problem isn't lack of information. It's lack of **filtering, framing, and focus**.

And that's where ChatGPT becomes your research superpower.

Used correctly, ChatGPT doesn't just give you *facts*. It helps you form **better questions**, summarize faster, and think more critically. Instead of drowning in data, you learn how to **surf the waves of knowledge**—confidently and with purpose.

In this chapter, you'll learn how to:

- Use ChatGPT for faster, smarter research
- Ask layered questions that get to the heart of a topic
- Avoid misinformation traps and generic answers

- Use AI to guide—not replace—your curiosity

Let's dive in.

ChatGPT ≠ Google (And Why That Matters)

Many people try to use ChatGPT like a search engine. They ask things like:

> *"What's the capital of Brazil?"*
> *"Who won the Super Bowl in 1999?"*
> *"What's the best productivity app?"*

And sure, it *can* answer those questions—but that's not where it shines.

Google gives you **links**. ChatGPT gives you **language**. It explains. It summarizes. It compares. It interprets. It **helps you think** through what you find.

Instead of searching for isolated facts, ChatGPT is best used for:

- Synthesizing information across multiple perspectives
- Explaining complex topics in simple terms
- Asking follow-up questions in a conversational flow
- Identifying the "so what" behind raw data

Think of it like this:

> ***Google helps you find information. ChatGPT helps you make sense of it.***

That's a huge distinction—and a huge advantage.

Use Case: Speed Research on Any Topic

Let's say you want to learn about a new topic—say, **the future of renewable energy**—but you're starting from scratch.

Step 1: Start Broad

> *"Give me a basic overview of the current state of renewable energy and where it's headed in the next 10 years."*

ChatGPT gives you a summary: solar, wind, policy shifts, emerging tech, etc.

Step 2: Zoom In

> *"What are the biggest challenges facing solar energy right now?"*
> *"Compare wind and geothermal energy in terms of cost and scalability."*

Now you're getting insight.

Step 3: Add Perspective

> *"What would a fossil fuel executive say about this trend?"*
> *"What's one argument against rapid renewable adoption, and how might an expert respond?"*

Now you're thinking critically.

Step 4: Apply It

> *"I'm writing a LinkedIn post for professionals in clean tech. Summarize this trend in 3 bullet points using accessible language."*

You've just gone from curious to *competent*—in minutes.

The Secret to Smarter Research: Ask Smarter Questions

When you ask ChatGPT a vague or overly general question, the answer will usually disappoint you.

Bad:

> *"Tell me about leadership."*
> *"How do I get better at time management?"*
> *"What are some business ideas?"*

Better:

> *"What are 3 uncommon leadership traits that are often overlooked in startup founders?"*
> *"What are the most common time management mistakes people make when working remotely?"*
> *"Give me 5 niche business ideas in the outdoor gear space for Gen Z consumers."*

Great questions generate great thinking. And ChatGPT can help you **develop** those questions, too.

Try asking:

- "What's a better way to phrase this question?"
- "What would a more specific version of this question look like?"
- "Can you help me ask a smarter question about [topic]?"

You're training yourself to become a **better researcher and thinker** just by prompting better.

The "Question Ladder" Technique

Use this method to climb from basic understanding to deep insight:

1. **Surface Question:** "What is digital transformation?"
2. **Contextual Question:** "Why is digital transformation important for small businesses?"
3. **Comparative Question:** "How does digital transformation differ between healthcare and retail?"
4. **Critical Question:** "What are the hidden costs or draw-backs of rapid digital transformation?"
5. **Strategic Question:** "If I were a consultant, how could I help a small business go digital without overwhelming them?"

Each step moves you deeper into expertise—and ChatGPT can help answer every layer.

Avoiding Shallow or Incorrect Information

Let's be honest: ChatGPT isn't perfect. It can:

- "Hallucinate" (make things up with confidence)
- Reference outdated info (especially on current events)
- Miss nuance or contradict itself

Here's how to minimize those issues:

Ask for Sources or Origin

> *"Where did this information come from?"*
> *"Can you list the original sources this is based on?"*
> *"Was this part of your training data or is this a guess?"*

If the answer is vague or it admits uncertainty, **verify it independently**.

Cross-Check with Google

Use ChatGPT to find a frame or summary, then search the real-time data on Google, PubMed, YouTube, or news sources.

Specify Timeframe

> *"Summarize the top AI breakthroughs between 2022 and 2024."*
> *"What were the most important news stories in the mental health space in the past 12 months?"*

ChatGPT may not always have the *most* current data—but it can synthesize what it was trained on remarkably well.

Use ChatGPT to Create Research Summaries and Cheat Sheets

If you're diving into a new field—marketing, history, nutrition, UX design—you can ask ChatGPT to act as your personal research assistant.

Prompt Examples:

- "Act like a tutor. Summarize the key ideas of cognitive behavioral therapy in 5 bullet points."
- "Give me a cheat sheet on search engine optimization, with terms and definitions."
- "What are the most important frameworks in negotiation theory?"
- "Make a table comparing the pros and cons of email marketing vs. paid ads."

You can even ask:

> *"Quiz me on what I just learned."*
> *"Explain it to me using a metaphor."*
> *"Make this sound like a tweet."*
> *"Summarize it for a 10-year-old."*

This isn't just faster research. It's **active learning.**

Rapid Research Prompt Templates

Here's a go-to set of prompts you can use for quick, focused exploration:

- "Summarize [topic] like I'm brand new to it."
- "What are the 3 main schools of thought on [issue]?"
- "Compare [X] and [Y] in a table."
- "What's a contrarian view on this subject?"
- "What common assumptions are wrong about this idea?"
- "How would a beginner vs. expert explain this differently?"
- "What would a smart follow-up question be to this idea?"

Each of these can take you from passive reader to **engaged thinker**.

Build a Thinking Habit with AI-Assisted Curiosity

Here's a powerful practice: anytime you find yourself reading or watching something interesting—pause, and feed it into ChatGPT.

> *"I just read this article about burnout. Can you summarize the key points for me?"*
>
> *"I watched a YouTube video on Stoicism. What questions should I be asking to understand it deeper?"*
>
> *"This podcast mentioned a trend in AI and healthcare. Can you explain that trend with examples?"*

You're now using AI not just to consume—but to **process and internalize**.

This is how you build a thinking habit. You turn information into knowledge—and knowledge into wisdom.

Recap: Fast Research. Smart Thinking.

Let's recap the core lessons of this chapter:

- ChatGPT is not Google—it's your **thinking assistant**, not your search engine
- Ask *better* questions, not just faster ones
- Use the "Question Ladder" to go from surface to strategy
- Beware of AI hallucinations—always verify with trusted sources
- Use AI to generate summaries, cheat sheets, comparisons, and metaphors
- Turn passive research into **interactive exploration**

When you stop trying to memorize everything and start **collaborating with your curiosity**, you free up mental energy to do your best thinking.

In the next chapter, we'll shift gears and explore **mental models on demand**—how to use ChatGPT to apply classic decision-making and problem-solving frameworks to your real-life challenges.

Let's keep thinking sharper, faster, and more creatively.

7

Mental Models on Demand

If you want to think faster and smarter, you don't just need more *information.*

You need better *frameworks.*

That's what mental models are: **reusable thinking tools** that help you understand, evaluate, and act more clearly. They're shortcuts for reasoning—like having a toolbox full of mental "lenses" you can pull out to make sense of complex problems, avoid common pitfalls, and make better decisions faster.

Think of them as:

- Patterns that help you see the invisible structure behind problems
- Strategies to avoid traps like overthinking or bias
- Mental scaffolding to organize messy situations

And here's the good news:

You don't have to memorize them all.

You can ask ChatGPT to **apply** them for you—on demand.

In this chapter, you'll learn:

- What mental models are and why they matter
- How to use ChatGPT to think through problems using powerful models
- Examples of popular models applied to real-life situations
- Prompt formulas for leveraging them whenever you're stuck, overwhelmed, or uncertain

Let's dive into the mental model superpower you didn't know you had.

What Are Mental Models?

A mental model is simply a **way of thinking about how something works**. It's a conceptual framework that helps you make sense of the world.

Some models are based on science (e.g., second-order effects).

Some are rooted in psychology (e.g., confirmation bias).

Others come from business, math, economics, or philosophy.

You already use them every day—even if you don't name them.

For example:

- When you take a step back and ask, "What's the worst that could happen?" you're using **inversion**.
- When you realize that a small input led to a big result, you're using the **Pareto Principle** (80/20 rule).
- When you decide *not* to act until you gather more info, you're applying **first principles thinking** or **probabilistic reasoning**.

The more you use these models, the more *efficient and accurate* your thinking becomes.

But instead of trying to learn all 100+ models yourself, you can ask ChatGPT to:

- Suggest one
- Apply one
- Explain one
- Compare a few
- Walk you through one step-by-step

This turns your AI tool into a **decision-making coach and problem-solving partner.**

How Mental Models Help You Think Faster

Imagine this:

You're facing a big decision. You're overwhelmed. Your brain is spinning with emotion, data, and possible scenarios.

Instead of asking, "What should I do?"—which often leads to vague answers—you ask ChatGPT:

> *"Use the Eisenhower Matrix to help me sort my current task list."*

Now you're not just reacting. You're **thinking within a proven structure**.

That's the power of models:

- They reduce cognitive load
- They give shape to chaos

- They help you ask better follow-up questions
- They *accelerate* clarity

Let's look at how to use ChatGPT to apply them with precision.

The "Model on Demand" Prompt Formula

Here's the simple formula:

"Apply [mental model] to [situation] and explain it like I'm [experience level or context]."

You can also ask:

- "What mental models are useful for [problem]?"
- "Explain [model] with a real-life example."
- "Compare [model A] vs. [model B] in this context."
- "Walk me through a decision using [model]."

This unlocks *immediate* insight. No need to remember or master every model. ChatGPT becomes your ready-to-use **thinking toolkit**.

Example 1: Inversion for Clarity

You say:

> *"I'm trying to build a more productive morning routine, but I keep getting distracted."*

Try this prompt:

> *"Use inversion to help me identify what* not *to do if I*

> *want my mornings to be focused and productive."*

ChatGPT might reply:

- Don't check your phone first thing
- Don't start without a plan from the night before
- Don't skip sleep the night before
- Don't stack too many tasks or goals into one morning
- Don't expect motivation to magically show up

Suddenly, your clarity increases—not by adding things, but by subtracting the wrong ones.

That's inversion in action.

And it took seconds.

Example 2: Second-Order Thinking for Planning

You say:

> *"I'm thinking of quitting my job to freelance full-time, but I'm nervous."*

Prompt:

> *"Use second-order thinking to explore the potential ripple effects of quitting my job to go freelance."*

ChatGPT might explore:

- First-order: more freedom, more risk, variable income

- Second-order: need for self-discipline, possible tax complications, impact on savings, change in social dynamics, long-term career implications

Now you're seeing **beyond the first wave of outcomes.** You're thinking strategically.

Example 3: First Principles Thinking for Problem Solving

You say:

> *"I want to start a YouTube channel, but I feel overwhelmed by all the advice out there."*

Prompt:

> *"Use first principles thinking to help me simplify my approach to starting a YouTube channel."*

ChatGPT breaks it down:

1. What is a YouTube channel? A place to share videos online.
2. Why do people subscribe? Value, consistency, relatability.
3. What do I need? A niche, basic equipment, a publishing schedule, an editing method.
4. What's *essential*? Making videos people care about, not fancy gear.

You've just simplified the complex by returning to fundamentals.

This clears the path forward.

10 Popular Mental Models You Can Prompt ChatGPT To Use

Here's a starter pack:

Model	Use it for...
Inversion	Avoiding failure by thinking backward
First Principles	Simplifying complex problems
Second-Order Thinking	Anticipating unintended consequences
Pareto Principle (80/20)	Focusing on what matters most
Eisenhower Matrix	Prioritizing tasks
Occam's Razor	Choosing the simplest explanation
Confirmation Bias	Challenging your assumptions
Probabilistic Thinking	Making better risk decisions
The Map is Not the Territory	Understanding the difference between models and reality
Circle of Competence	Knowing what you know—and what you don't

You can ask ChatGPT:

- "What does [model] mean?"
- "When should I use it?"
- "What's an example of this model in real life?"
- "How does this model apply to [my situation]?"

Thinking Better With Model Stacking

What's better than one mental model?

Two or three used together.

This is called **model stacking**—and ChatGPT can do it for you.

Try prompts like:

- "Use both the 80/20 rule and second-order thinking to help me prioritize my business goals."
- "Combine inversion and Occam's Razor to troubleshoot this issue I'm having with my website."
- "What models would work well *together* to evaluate a major career change?"

This approach blends multiple lenses to give you a **richer view of your problem.** It's like consulting a team of brilliant thinkers—all instantly, in one place.

Model Builder Prompts to Try Today

Here are prompt starters you can personalize:

1. "Act as a decision coach. Apply the Eisenhower Matrix to my current to-do list, which includes [list tasks]."
2. "I'm torn between two business ideas. Help me evaluate them using first principles thinking."
3. "Use the 80/20 rule to help me streamline my social media strategy as a solopreneur."
4. "What mental models could help me design a better on-boarding process for new clients?"
5. "Explain the difference between correlation and causation

using a parenting example."
6. "What's a mental model that helps with imposter syndrome? How can I apply it to my job search?"

These aren't just prompts. They're **thinking frameworks** disguised as questions.

Caution: Don't Over-Rely on a Single Model

Mental models are tools, not truth.

Like a hammer, they're useful—but not for every problem. If you only ever apply inversion, you'll miss the upsides. If you only ever use first principles, you may over-simplify complex realities.

The goal isn't to find *one perfect model.*

It's to build a **mental toolbox**—and use the right tool at the right time.

ChatGPT helps you do this faster than ever. It doesn't get tired. It doesn't roll its eyes when you ask a "dumb" question. It's the ideal thinking partner for trying on new models and testing out new ideas.

Recap: Mental Models Make Thinking Faster, Sharper, and Smarter

Let's review what you've learned:

- Mental models are reusable thinking tools that simplify decision-making
- You can ask ChatGPT to **apply**, **explain**, or **compare** models to your situation

- Popular models like inversion, first principles, and second-order thinking can transform your clarity
- "Model stacking" combines multiple perspectives for deeper insight
- Don't rely on one lens—use the right model for the problem

Mental models are like cognitive power tools. With ChatGPT as your assistant, you don't have to memorize or master them—you just need to **know when and how to ask for one**.

In the next chapter, we'll shift gears into **rapid summarization and comprehension**—how to use ChatGPT to turn long content into instant clarity, so you never have to feel overwhelmed by information again.

Let's keep thinking sharper—and lighter.

8

Speed Reading for Your Brain

We're swimming in content.

Books. Emails. Reports. Articles. Podcasts. Transcripts. Social media threads. Course materials. White papers. Webinars.

If you're like most people, there's a growing pile of things you *meant* to read, *should* understand, or *need* to get through... someday.

The problem isn't lack of motivation. It's **information overload**. We're trying to drink from a firehose. And in that rush, we either skim everything or give up altogether.

But what if there was a way to **read faster, comprehend more, and retain only what matters**—without losing nuance or context?

That's what this chapter is all about.

ChatGPT, when used strategically, becomes your **speed-reading sidekick**. It can:

- Summarize dense text in seconds
- Pull out key takeaways
- Reframe the content in plain language

- Turn articles into outlines, transcripts into action plans, and info-dumps into clarity

It's not about skipping understanding. It's about accelerating *to* understanding.

Let's explore how to use ChatGPT as your personal fast-lane to knowledge.

The Problem with Traditional Reading

Here's a familiar cycle:

1. You open a long article or report.
2. You start strong but begin skimming.
3. You finish with a vague sense of the topic—and forget most of it a day later.
4. You save the link, telling yourself you'll "re-read it when you have time." (You won't.)

Or you want to "study" something:

- You watch a YouTube video but zone out halfway.
- You sign up for a course but never finish it.
- You try to take notes but don't know what's important.

The issue isn't attention span—it's *lack of a filtering mechanism.* Without a guide, everything seems equally important. Your brain gets overwhelmed and disengages.

That's where ChatGPT changes the game. It becomes your **real-time filter, explainer, and note-taker**—all rolled into one.

What ChatGPT Can Do with Long Content

Here's what's possible when you combine long-form content with the right ChatGPT prompts:

- Summarize a 2,000-word blog post into 5 bullet points
- Turn a 10-page research report into a 3-paragraph explainer
- Extract the action steps from a 60-minute podcast
- Rephrase technical jargon in plain English
- Identify the most important statistics, arguments, or quotes
- Create a quiz to reinforce what you learned
- Turn lecture notes into a visual outline or study guide

And it all happens in *seconds*—with **zero skimming or rewinding on your part**.

This doesn't just save time. It **boosts confidence and comprehension**.

The Speed Reading Prompt Formula

Here's your go-to template:

> *"Summarize the following [article, chapter, transcript] into [format: bullet points, outline, paragraph], focusing on [goal: key takeaways, action steps, arguments, etc.]. Use clear, simple language."*

You can also ask:

- "What's the main argument here?"
- "Who is the intended audience?"
- "What are the strengths and weaknesses of this piece?"
- "Give me 3 questions this raises or leaves unanswered."
- "Rephrase this for a high school reader."

Let's walk through a real example.

Example: Summarizing an Article

Let's say you paste in an article titled:
"The Future of Remote Work in a Post-Pandemic World"
Prompt:

> *"Summarize this article in 5 bullet points that focus on how remote work is affecting companies long term. Keep the language simple and clear."*

ChatGPT replies:

1. Many companies are shifting to hybrid work models to balance flexibility and collaboration.
2. Real estate costs are decreasing as companies reduce physical office space.
3. Productivity has increased in some industries but decreased in others.
4. Companies are rethinking how to measure performance and manage teams.
5. Employee well-being and burnout are becoming major concerns in remote settings.

Now you don't need to read 2,000 words to get the core insights. You've extracted what matters most—instantly.

Customizing Your Summary Style

Depending on your needs, you can ask ChatGPT to change the tone, structure, or format of the summary.

Try:

- "Summarize this like a professor teaching a college class."
- "Turn this into a social media thread with 5 punchy tweets."
- "Make this sound like a TED Talk opener."
- "Write this as if explaining it to a 10-year-old."
- "Create a one-page cheat sheet from this content."

ChatGPT can match the **voice, length, and complexity level** you need.

What About Books?

Books can be challenging to summarize—but incredibly rewarding. You don't want to reduce a great book to a list of takeaways, but sometimes, you need:

- A refresher
- A quick decision on whether to read it
- A tool to help you *retain* what you've already read

Try prompts like:

> *"Give me a 3-paragraph summary of the book* Deep

Work *by Cal Newport."*

"List the 5 most important lessons from Atomic Habits *by James Clear."*

"Explain the key message of Man's Search for Meaning *in plain language."*

You can also copy/paste a chapter or excerpt and say:

"Summarize this section in an outline so I can use it in a presentation."

"Highlight any metaphors or quotes I should remember."

"What's the author's main argument here?"

You'll retain more—and spend less time re-reading.

Podcasts, Videos, and Transcripts

If you're someone who learns by watching or listening, you'll love this:

ChatGPT can digest *transcripts* of:

- Podcasts
- Webinars
- Interviews
- YouTube videos
- Lectures or panel discussions

Prompt:

"Here's the transcript from a podcast about burnout.

Summarize it in 6 bullet points, then give me 2 follow-up questions I could ask myself."

Or:

"Create an outline of this 45-minute video transcript, separating each section by topic. Label the transitions clearly."

You can even say:

"Pretend I'm giving a presentation on this interview. Give me 3 key quotes to use and why they matter."

Suddenly, your passive listening becomes **active insight extraction**.

Extracting for Learning and Retention

Don't just summarize—**personalize**. You can use ChatGPT to turn content into *learning tools*:

Flashcards

"Turn this article into 10 flashcards using Q&A format."

Memory Hooks

"Give me a metaphor or story that helps me remember this concept."

Quiz

> *"Create a 5-question quiz based on this material."*

Action Plan

> *"Based on this content, what are 3 things I can apply this week?"*

The more you interact with the material using ChatGPT, the **deeper it sticks**.

Rapid Summary Prompts You Can Use Today

Here's a toolkit of ready-to-go prompts:

1. "Summarize this article in 5 bullet points for a beginner audience."
2. "What are the most important facts, stats, or trends from this document?"
3. "Turn this into a checklist I can use to implement the ideas."
4. "Rephrase this so it sounds more inspiring and engaging."
5. "Explain the main idea of this text using a cooking metaphor."
6. "Compare the two arguments made in this essay and list their pros/cons."
7. "Extract any key quotes or memorable phrases from this speech."

These prompts help you **consume less and learn more**.

What to Watch Out For

Don't Use AI as Your Only Source

ChatGPT can misinterpret or oversimplify. Always skim the original content when stakes are high.

Be Aware of Missing Context

If you copy/paste only part of a conversation or text, the AI won't have full context. Either include a preface or summarize what's missing.

Don't Memorize—Engage

Summaries are helpful, but true understanding comes from *applying* what you learn. Use prompts that help you relate the content to your life or goals.

Recap: Accelerate Your Understanding

Let's bring it home:

- ChatGPT is your **speed-reading ally**—helping you summarize, rephrase, and extract insights from any content
- Use it to turn long, dense materials into **bullet points, outlines, or cheat sheets**
- Prompt for specific tone, voice, and format (TED Talk, Q&A, metaphor, etc.)
- Extract ideas, arguments, quotes, actions, and follow-up questions

- Turn passive consumption into **active, personalized learning**

You no longer need to read *everything* to understand *anything*.

In the next chapter, we'll explore how to **use ChatGPT to make faster, more confident decisions** by mapping out options, weighing consequences, and avoiding common cognitive traps.

Let's keep the momentum going.

9

Decision Sprinting with ChatGPT

We make thousands of decisions every day—from what to eat for lunch to whether to switch careers, launch a new product, or take a risk that could change everything.

Some decisions are small. Some feel huge. But most share one thing in common:

> ***They're harder than they need to be.***

Why?

Because we overthink. We get stuck in loops. We worry about missing out, failing, or choosing the wrong path. And when the stakes are high, we often default to *inaction*.

But what if you didn't have to make those decisions alone?

What if you had a thinking partner who could help you sort options, challenge your assumptions, and weigh the ripple effects—fast?

That's exactly how you can use ChatGPT: **as your decision sprint coach**.

In this chapter, you'll learn how to:

- Use ChatGPT to break complex choices into clear, actionable parts
- Compare options using frameworks and mental models
- Avoid common decision-making traps (like paralysis or perfectionism)
- Move forward with more clarity and less second-guessing

Whether you're stuck on what to prioritize today or navigating a life-changing fork in the road, this chapter will give you tools to decide faster—and smarter.

Why We Get Stuck When Making Decisions

Most people think the problem is **not knowing what to choose**.
But more often, the real blockers are:

- **Too many choices** (choice overload)
- **Fear of regret** (what if I choose wrong?)
- **Perfectionism** (waiting for the perfect option)
- **Lack of structure** (no system to guide the process)

In other words: it's not about *information*. It's about *overload* and *uncertainty*.
ChatGPT can help you clear both by providing:

- Structure to think through your options
- Prompts to explore consequences and priorities
- Reframes to reduce anxiety and bias

Let's walk through how.

ChatGPT as a Decision Sprint Partner

A **decision sprint** is a fast, focused burst of intentional thinking. Instead of endlessly weighing every possibility, you move through a simple 5-step framework—quickly and clearly—with AI as your co-pilot.

Here's how it works.

Step 1: Define the Decision

Prompt:

> *"Help me clarify the decision I'm trying to make."*

Why it works: Many times, you're not stuck because the options are bad—you're stuck because the *real question* hasn't been defined.

Example:

You start with: "I don't know if I should leave my job."

ChatGPT might clarify:

> *"You're trying to decide whether staying in your current job aligns with your long-term career goals, financial needs, and personal well-being. Is that correct?"*

Already, things feel more focused.

Step 2: List the Options

Prompt:

> *"What are 3 to 5 possible options related to this decision—including ones I might not be considering?"*

Why it works: We often limit ourselves to a binary ("Should I do this or not?") when there are actually **multiple paths** worth exploring.

Example:
ChatGPT might say:

1. Stay in your current role and make it work
2. Switch to a similar role at a new company
3. Take a career break or sabbatical
4. Transition to freelancing or consulting
5. Start applying now and give yourself a decision deadline

Now you're thinking expansively, not reactively.

Step 3: Compare and Evaluate

Prompt:

> *"Create a pros and cons list for each option."*

You can also ask:

- "What are the long-term consequences of each choice?"
- "Which one aligns most with my values or goals?"

- "Which one has the most second-order effects I need to consider?"

ChatGPT returns organized insights, like:

Option	Pros	Cons
Stay in current job	Stability, known environment, benefits	Burnout, limited growth
Switch jobs	New challenges, possibly better culture	Uncertainty, risk of repeat issues
Sabbatical	Rest, clarity, personal reset	Financial strain, resume gap

Now you can see trade-offs—without swirling in ambiguity.

Step 4: Use a Framework

This is where you bring in structure to avoid bias or impulse.

Use the Eisenhower Matrix

Prompt:

> *"Sort these tasks by urgency and importance to help me decide what to do today."*

Use the Weighted Decision Matrix

Prompt:

> *"Create a decision matrix comparing [Option A, B, C] across factors like cost, time, impact, and alignment with*

my values."

Use Regret Minimization

Prompt:

> *"Help me apply Jeff Bezos's 'Regret Minimization Framework' to this choice."*

ChatGPT replies:

> *"Imagine you're 80 years old looking back—will you regret not trying this? If so, the cost of inaction may be higher than the cost of risk."*

This reframing can be powerful. It gives you a new lens—and the emotional distance—to act.

Step 5: Create a Plan (or Next Step)

Prompt:

> *"What's the smallest first step I could take toward this choice?"*

ChatGPT might respond:

> *"Start by writing a one-paragraph vision of what success looks like in 6 months if you choose this path. Then make a list of what you'd need to research or prepare."*

Momentum reduces fear. And fear is often the biggest roadblock to clear decision-making.

Bonus: Use ChatGPT for Role-Play

This is one of the most powerful (and underused) tools.

Prompt:

> *"Pretend you're my future self, one year after I made this decision. Tell me how things turned out."*

Or:

> *"Play devil's advocate. What would someone skeptical of this option say?"*

Or:

> *"Act as a mentor or coach. What advice would you give me about this choice?"*

These prompts give you **fresh perspective**—without needing to consult 10 different people. You get clarity now.

Use Cases: Real Decisions, Real Prompts

Here are some real-life decisions you can speed up with ChatGPT:

Career Pivot

> *"Help me compare staying at my job vs. going back to school using a long-term lens."*

Product Launch

> *"What are the second-order effects of launching this product now vs. later?"*

Relationship Choice

> *"Use the 80/20 rule to assess what's working and what's draining me in this relationship."*

Big Purchase

> *"What factors should I weigh before buying a house in this market? Give me a checklist."*

Life Design

> *"What would be the most energy-giving choice for my long-term well-being?"*

Avoiding Decision Traps with AI

Let's call out a few traps—and how ChatGPT can help you avoid them.

Perfectionism

Trap: *"I need to find the* perfect *option."*
Fix: *Ask:*
"What's a 'good enough' decision I could make that moves me forward today?"

Analysis Paralysis

Trap: *"I'm overthinking every detail."*
Fix: *Ask:*
"What are the 3 most important factors to focus on, and what can I ignore for now?"

Over-Reliance on Emotion

Trap: *"I feel nervous, so I must be making a mistake."*
Fix: *Ask:*
"What are the facts vs. the fears in this situation?"

Binary Thinking

Trap: *"It's either this or that."*
Fix: *Ask:*
"What's a third or fourth option I haven't considered yet?"

ChatGPT can help you shift from **reaction to reflection**—and from hesitation to action.

Recap: Sprint, Don't Spin

Decision-making doesn't have to be agonizing.

With the right tools and prompts, it can be **swift, strategic, and satisfying.**

Here's your Decision Sprint Checklist:

1. **Clarify the question** you're really asking
2. **List options** (including ones you may not have seen)
3. **Compare trade-offs** using pros/cons or mental models
4. **Use a framework** (regret minimization, Eisenhower, etc.)
5. **Choose or act**—even if it's just the smallest first step
6. **Check your blind spots** with role-play or devil's advocate prompts

You don't need to get it perfect. You just need to get moving—with clarity.

And now, you've got a tool that can help you make **dozens of smarter decisions a week**—without burning out your brain.

In the next chapter, we'll tackle one of the most common enemies of momentum: **mental blocks**. You'll learn how to use ChatGPT to beat procrastination, analysis paralysis, and creative freeze with fast, practical prompts.

Let's keep thinking—and acting—faster.

10

Overcome Mental Blocks Instantly

We all get stuck.

You sit down to write, and nothing comes out.

You look at your task list and feel frozen.

You think about starting a new project—but suddenly decide to clean the kitchen instead.

This is the experience of a **mental block**. It's not about laziness or lack of discipline. It's about friction: a buildup of emotional and cognitive tension that clouds your ability to move forward.

Some blocks show up as:

- **Procrastination** ("I'll do it later... maybe.")
- **Perfectionism** ("It's not ready yet.")
- **Analysis paralysis** ("There are too many options.")
- **Creative freeze** ("I can't think of anything good.")

These aren't personal failures. They're human patterns.

And the good news is: **they're solvable—quickly**—with the right tools.

In this chapter, you'll learn how to use ChatGPT as a **block-breaker**. You'll discover prompts that unlock action, reduce pressure, and restore clarity when your brain feels jammed.

Whether you're facing a blank page, a big decision, or just can't seem to get started, these strategies will help you get unstuck—and keep moving.

What Causes Mental Blocks?

Before we bust them, let's understand them.

Most mental blocks come from one of these sources:

1. **Fear** – of failure, judgment, looking stupid, wasting time
2. **Overwhelm** – too much to do, too little clarity, unclear next steps
3. **Pressure** – to be perfect, original, fast, brilliant
4. **Confusion** – not knowing where to start or what matters most
5. **Disconnection** – forgetting why something matters or losing energy for it

These triggers activate your inner resistance. Your brain wants to protect you, so it says, *"Let's just avoid this for now."*

That's where ChatGPT can help—not by forcing action, but by reducing friction. By lowering the mental load, clarifying the next step, and making progress feel safe, ChatGPT helps you *start.*

And once you start, momentum does the rest.

ChatGPT as Your Unblocker-in-Chief

Let's reframe ChatGPT.

It's not just a chatbot. It's your:

- **Anti-procrastination coach**
- **Gentle creative partner**
- **Brainstorming buddy**
- **Task untangler**
- **Motivation mirror**

When you're stuck, you can literally *type your stuckness into the box*—and let ChatGPT help you break it apart.

Let's walk through the most common blocks—and the prompts to shatter them.

BLOCK 1: "I Don't Know Where to Start"

This is one of the most common traps. You know what you want to do... but the beginning feels fuzzy, intimidating, or overwhelming.

Try this prompt:

> *"I want to [insert goal], but I don't know where to start. Can you help me break it into small, doable steps?"*

Example:

> *"I want to start a blog about parenting, but I don't know where to begin."*

ChatGPT might reply:

1. Choose a niche or theme (e.g., toddlers, single parenting, parenting teens)
2. Brainstorm 5 blog post ideas
3. Pick one and write a rough outline
4. Choose a platform (Medium, WordPress, Substack)
5. Publish your first post—even if it's short

Suddenly, your mountain becomes a staircase. You can see the first step—and that's enough to begin.

BLOCK 2: "It Has to Be Perfect"

Ah, perfectionism—the elegant excuse that keeps creators stuck forever.

When you feel like nothing is good enough to start, publish, or share, you can prompt ChatGPT to help you **loosen your grip.**

Try:

> *"Pretend you're a kind but honest writing coach. Remind me why perfectionism is the enemy of progress."*

Or:

> *"Give me permission to write something messy. Help me embrace a 'rough draft' mindset."*

Or:

> *"I'm writing a first draft. Help me write a version that's good enough to improve later."*

Example Output:

> *"The first draft isn't meant to be perfect—it's meant to exist. Every great article, book, or script starts out messy. You can't edit a blank page, but you can improve a rough one. Let's get something down. Then we'll polish it."*

Now you're no longer aiming for perfect. You're aiming for *possible*. That's the win.

BLOCK 3: "I Can't Think of Any Ideas"

Creative freeze usually comes from fear of being boring, wrong, or cliché. The pressure to be original strangles spontaneity.

Let ChatGPT generate the first spark. You can shape it from there.

Try:

> *"Give me 10 unexpected angles on the topic of [X]."*
>
> *"Brainstorm rough ideas for a [blog post / video / tweet / talk] about [topic]."*
>
> *"What are some metaphors I could use to explain [concept]?"*
>
> *"I'm stuck creatively. Can you ask me 3 questions to get me thinking?"*

Example:

> *"Give me blog post angles on 'discipline for creative people.'"*

ChatGPT replies:

1. "Why Creative Burnout Isn't a Time Problem—It's a Discipline Problem"
2. "The Myth of the Tortured Artist: What Happens When You Add Structure to Genius"
3. "5 Daily Rituals That Fuel Consistent Creativity (Without Killing Your Soul)"

You don't have to use them all. But even *one* idea can open the floodgates.

BLOCK 4: "I Have Too Many Ideas and Can't Choose"

This is the flip side of creative freeze: **creative overwhelm**.

ChatGPT can help you **sort, rank, and reduce** your options until you feel clear.

Try:

> *"Here are 10 ideas I'm considering. Help me narrow them down to 3 based on [impact / time / excitement / audience need]."*
>
> *"Create a decision matrix comparing these ideas across urgency and long-term value."*
>
> *"Ask me questions that help me clarify which idea I'm most energized by."*

Suddenly, the mental noise gets organized. You're no longer choosing between 10 scattered ideas—you're choosing from 3 focused, aligned options.

That's clarity. That's progress.

BLOCK 5: "I Feel Unmotivated or Disconnected"

Sometimes the problem isn't the task. It's your *why*.

You've lost touch with the purpose behind the project. Or you're tired. Or it just feels too far away to care.

That's when ChatGPT becomes your **motivation mirror**.

Try:

> *"Remind me why I started working on this project in the first place."*
>
> *"Ask me 3 questions to reconnect me to the purpose of this work."*
>
> *"Help me write a short vision statement for this project—why it matters and who it helps."*
>
> *"Write me a 3-sentence pep talk to remind me that small progress counts."*

Example Pep Talk:

> *"Progress isn't about massive leaps—it's about showing up when it would be easier not to. You're building something real, one decision at a time. The fact that you're here means you haven't given up. Keep going."*

You don't need fake hype. You need real connection to your

purpose. ChatGPT can help you find your footing again.

More Unblocker Prompts to Try Anytime

Here's a rapid-fire list of prompts for specific stuck moments:

- "I'm procrastinating. What's the smallest step I could take right now?"
- "Give me a 5-minute version of this task so I can at least start."
- "I feel overwhelmed. Help me break this into 3 smaller chunks."
- "I'm afraid of failing. Give me a reframe that makes failure less scary."
- "Turn this massive to-do into a 3-step 'minimum viable task' list."
- "Write me a 1-paragraph sloppy first draft so I can build from it."
- "Ask me 3 questions to help me get unstuck."

Use these like flashcards for your brain. They *move energy*. That's the key.

Recap: Get Unstuck, On Demand

Let's bring it all together.

Common Blocks:

- "I don't know where to start."
- "It's not good enough."
- "I have no ideas."
- "I have too many ideas."
- "I lost motivation."

ChatGPT Solutions:

- Break down the first step
- Embrace imperfection
- Spark ideas and reframe pressure
- Prioritize and simplify
- Reconnect to purpose

Mental blocks aren't problems. They're signals.

They're not signs of weakness. They're **opportunities to work with your mind**, not against it.

ChatGPT helps you *externalize* those thoughts. It gives you a fresh angle, a softer tone, a nudge forward—instantly.

The next time you feel stuck, don't wait.

Just type what you're feeling—and let your thinking partner help you move again.

In the next chapter, we'll shift from blocks to **brainstorms**. You'll learn how to turn ChatGPT into a full-scale **idea engine**, generating dozens of usable, surprising, and creative ideas—without burnout.

Let's keep building momentum.

11

The Rapid Ideation Toolkit

There's nothing quite like a good idea at the right time.

The moment when inspiration strikes, your mind lights up, and momentum follows.

But let's be honest: those moments don't always show up when you need them.

Sometimes you sit down to brainstorm—and your brain just... doesn't.

No ideas.

No spark.

No flow.

This is the reality of **ideation under pressure**—whether you're a writer, marketer, entrepreneur, coach, or student. You're expected to come up with something original, useful, or clever... now.

That's where ChatGPT becomes a game-changer.

Used strategically, it transforms into a **high-powered idea engine**. One that generates dozens of options quickly, adapts to your goals, and helps you develop rough ideas into polished plans.

In this chapter, you'll build your **Rapid Ideation Toolkit**—a collection of techniques, prompts, and real-world use cases that let you brainstorm smarter and faster.

Whether you need blog post angles, product names, creative hooks, business concepts, or fresh ways to say something old, you'll have a system to generate brilliance on demand.

Why You Need an Ideation System

Coming up with ideas is easy when you're in the zone.

But creativity isn't always convenient. And the truth is:

> ***Creativity is a skill—not just a spark.***

You can build it like a muscle. And just like physical training, it helps to have:

- The right tools
- A consistent process
- A "spotter" to help when your brain gets tired

ChatGPT is that spotter. It gives you volume, variation, and velocity—fast. No waiting for inspiration. Just guided exploration and generative thinking at your fingertips.

Let's look at how to do that effectively.

The 3-Phase Rapid Ideation Framework

Here's the system we'll use in this chapter:

1. Generate - Use ChatGPT to produce a high volume of raw ideas

2. Refine - Shape, combine, or evolve the strongest ones

3. Activate - Choose one and build it into something usable

This works for:

- Content creation
- Product development
- Branding and naming
- Marketing campaigns
- Business strategy
- Public speaking
- Educational projects
- Storytelling and character design

The prompts we'll explore are flexible and customizable—designed to **spark your thinking, not replace it.**

Phase 1: Generate (Go for Volume)

The first rule of brainstorming? **Don't judge—just generate.**

The goal here is *quantity*, not perfection. Let ChatGPT flood you with raw material. You can shape it later.

General-Purpose Idea Prompts

- "Give me 25 ideas for [topic]. Don't worry if they're rough—just generate."
- "Brainstorm unusual angles for a piece of content on [X]."
- "What are some provocative or contrarian takes on [subject]?"
- "What metaphors or analogies could explain [concept] in a fresh way?"
- "If I were launching a course on [topic], what would be some unexpected titles or angles?"

Niche Examples

For marketers:

> *"Brainstorm 10 unique campaign ideas for a skincare brand targeting eco-conscious Gen Z customers."*

For writers:

> *"Give me 15 opening lines for a cozy mystery novel set in a bookstore."*

For coaches/consultants:

> *"List 20 pain points my ideal client might experience before hiring someone like me."*

For educators:

> *"What are 10 creative ways to teach the concept of gravity to 5th graders?"*

The point is to overwhelm your inner critic with *too many* options to stay stuck.

Rapid Fire Idea Tools

Here are tools you can "load" into ChatGPT via prompts:

The List Generator

> *"List 100 content ideas related to [topic] for [target audience]."*

It doesn't matter if you use all 100. It matters that **you get out of your own head** and into flow.

The Reframe Machine

> *"Take this old idea—[paste in idea]—and give me 10 new ways to frame it for a modern audience."*

Great for reviving tired blog posts, taglines, slogans, or email subject lines.

The Role Reversal Prompt

> *"How would a [role: child, scientist, comedian, critic] explain or pitch this idea?"*

For example:

> *"How would a stand-up comedian pitch the benefits of financial planning?"*

This brings humor, perspective, and novelty to stale ideas.

The A-to-Z Challenge

> *"Give me one idea for each letter of the alphabet related to [topic]."*

Great for social posts, course modules, or creative exercises.

Phase 2: Refine (Sort the Gold)

Once you've got a pile of raw ideas, it's time to shape them.

Don't toss out ideas too quickly. Let ChatGPT help you evolve them.

Prompt Examples:

- "Combine idea 3 and idea 8 into a more focused concept."
- "Which of these ideas sounds most unique or emotionally engaging?"
- "Rewrite this idea to make it more niche-specific."
- "Turn this idea into a headline that would make someone stop scrolling."
- "Expand this concept into a 5-part series outline."

You can also add constraints:

"Reframe this idea so it appeals to time-starved entrepreneurs."

"Make this idea sound more playful and less corporate."

"Write this as if I'm speaking to a skeptical audience."

ChatGPT isn't just an idea machine—it's an idea *shaper.*

Phase 3: Activate (Build & Use)

Once you've selected a refined idea, the next step is **activation**—turning it into something real.

Ask ChatGPT to help you flesh it out:

- "Turn this idea into a blog post outline."
- "Create a script for a 60-second video based on this hook."
- "Give me a draft email introducing this idea to my audience."
- "What visuals could accompany this concept in a presentation?"
- "Turn this into a lead magnet idea with a title and description."

Now you've gone from *raw* → *refined* → *ready*—in minutes.

That's the power of thinking with an engine instead of white-knuckling it alone.

Smart Brainstorming Tactics

Use Constraints

Creativity thrives on limits. Tell ChatGPT to generate:

- "10 ideas under 100 characters"
- "Ideas that don't require any money to implement"
- "Ideas that use only analogies"
- "Names that start with the letter S"

You'll get sharper results—and more novelty.

Add Audience

Get specific. The prompt "blog post ideas about wellness" is okay... but:

> *"Give me blog post ideas about wellness for single dads in their 40s who work night shifts"* is *way better.*

Specificity focuses the lens. Use it.

Add Emotion or Tone

- "Make these ideas sound inspiring."
- "Add a sense of urgency."
- "Make this funny and self-deprecating."

Ideas aren't just logical—they're emotional. Lean into that.

The 5-Minute Idea Factory Prompt

When in doubt, use this "all-in-one" brainstorm jumpstart:

> *"Act like a creative strategist. I'm working on [project]. My audience is [describe them briefly]. Generate 15 ideas I could use to [goal: teach, persuade, engage, entertain]. Make the ideas varied in format and tone."*

You'll walk away with a full menu of options—plus the confidence to pick one and run with it.

Reuse, Remix, Reframe

Don't throw away old brainstorms.

Keep them. Revisit them. **Recycle them.**

Ask:

> *"What's a fresh way to use this old idea in a new format?"*
>
> *"How would I frame this idea for a different audience or industry?"*
>
> *"What would this look like as a challenge, a podcast episode, a tweet thread, or a workshop?"*

With ChatGPT, you're never out of ideas. You're just one great prompt away from a dozen more.

Recap: Build Your Idea Engine

Let's bring it all together.

Rapid Ideation Framework:

1. **Generate** – Go for volume without judgment
2. **Refine** – Shape, prioritize, and evolve strong concepts
3. **Activate** – Turn ideas into outlines, drafts, content, or campaigns

Tools to Use:

- List Generator
- Reframe Machine
- A-to-Z Challenge
- Role Reversal
- 5-Minute Idea Factory

Smart Tactics:

- Use constraints
- Add emotional tone
- Include audience details
- Don't throw away old ideas—remix them

You now have a **system for idea generation** that doesn't rely on waiting for inspiration. You can brainstorm anytime, for anything—with volume, clarity, and speed.

In the next chapter, we'll go even deeper into solving real-world problems. You'll learn how to use ChatGPT as a **problem-solving partner**—breaking down obstacles, exploring causes, and finding actionable solutions with confidence and creativity.

Let's keep thinking bigger—and faster.

12

The Problem Solver Protocol

Every day, you face problems that demand decisions. Some are simple—like handling an unexpected schedule change. Others are complex—like figuring out why a project stalled, how to fix a business bottleneck, or what's really behind a slump in motivation.

But here's the truth:

> ***Most people don't solve problems—they either avoid them or react to them.***

That's not because they're lazy or unmotivated. It's because real problem-solving takes mental clarity, emotional calm, and structured thinking—three things that are often hard to come by when you're stressed or stuck.

That's where ChatGPT comes in.

Used strategically, ChatGPT becomes your **diagnostic tool**, your **thought organizer**, and your **solution architect**. It helps you:

- Break a big mess into manageable pieces
- Uncover root causes instead of chasing symptoms
- Explore multiple approaches without pressure
- Evaluate pros, cons, and consequences
- Turn reflection into action—fast

This chapter introduces the **Problem Solver Protocol**: a clear, repeatable process that helps you work through nearly any challenge using AI as a calm, unbiased thinking partner.

Let's walk through it.

Step 1: Define the Problem Clearly

You can't solve what you haven't defined.

Many people start with vague frustration:

- "This isn't working."
- "I feel stuck."
- "Something's off."

That's valid—but not actionable.

Your first move? Ask ChatGPT to help you *articulate the real problem.*

Try:

> *"Help me define the problem I'm trying to solve. Here's what I know: [Insert your situation or frustration]."*
>
> *"What are 3 ways to rephrase this challenge so I can see it more clearly?"*
>
> *"What question should I really be asking here?"*

Example:

You say: "My product launch didn't do well."
ChatGPT might clarify:

> *"Are you trying to understand why the product didn't sell, or what to change for next time? Are you evaluating marketing, product-market fit, or customer experience?"*

Boom. You're no longer just feeling stuck—you're thinking diagnostically.

Step 2: Separate Symptoms from Root Causes

Once the problem is defined, the next challenge is focus. We often treat **symptoms** (what we can see) instead of **root causes** (what's really driving the issue).

ChatGPT can help you explore beneath the surface.

Try:

> *"Act like a business analyst. What are 5 possible root causes of this problem?"*
>
> *"Could this issue be a downstream effect of something else? Help me trace it back."*
>
> *"What patterns might I be missing here?"*

Example:

You say: "My team keeps missing deadlines."
ChatGPT might return:

- Poor scoping of work

- Lack of clarity in responsibilities
- Hidden bottlenecks in communication
- Overcommitment across too many projects
- Weak incentives or burnout

Now you have options. You're not solving the *wrong* problem—you're identifying leverage points.

Step 3: Reframe the Challenge

Sometimes the best way forward is to ask a *different question.*

ChatGPT is excellent at generating alternative frames that lead to insight.

Try:

> *"What's an unexpected way to look at this problem?"*
>
> *"If this were a puzzle, what would the missing piece be?"*
>
> *"How would a coach, investor, therapist, or competitor see this differently?"*
>
> *"What if the obstacle is actually a signal pointing me in a new direction?"*

This invites creativity. It softens mental rigidity.

Example:

"I'm not getting engagement on social media" becomes:

> *"Am I showing up consistently, or just posting randomly and hoping it sticks?"*

You've just reframed from "algorithm problem" to "strategy and behavior alignment."

That's progress.

Step 4: Generate Multiple Solutions

Don't stop at the first idea that comes to mind. Use ChatGPT to help you brainstorm multiple pathways.

Try:

> *"Give me 5 ways to solve this problem—from the simplest to the boldest."*
>
> *"What's a creative or counterintuitive solution I might not have considered?"*
>
> *"What would solving this look like without spending money?"*
>
> *"What's the fastest, lowest-risk way to test a possible solution?"*

Example Prompt:

> *"I'm getting unsubscribes from my newsletter. Suggest a few changes I could test to improve engagement before people drop off."*

ChatGPT might reply:

1. Add a short personal story to build connection
2. Simplify the formatting and reduce visual noise
3. Ask readers a one-question poll

4. Split test subject lines for curiosity vs. clarity
5. Reduce frequency and send only your best content

Now you're not just *hoping* things get better—you're taking specific action steps, backed by options.

Step 5: Evaluate Trade-Offs

Every solution comes with costs—time, money, complexity, emotional energy. ChatGPT can help you assess the trade-offs *before* you invest.

Try:

> *"What are the pros and cons of each solution?"*
> *"What might go wrong with each approach, and how could I prevent it?"*
> *"What are the long-term vs. short-term consequences?"*
> *"Which of these aligns best with my values or priorities?"*

Example:
You're considering hiring a virtual assistant.
Prompt:

> *"List the benefits, risks, and decision criteria to consider before hiring a VA for a solopreneur."*

ChatGPT might return:

- **Benefits:** Time saved, reduced task load, scalability
- **Risks:** Training required, potential for miscommunication, budget impact
- **Decision criteria:** Type of tasks, budget, desired hours/week, need for specialized skills

You now have a decision framework—not just a gut feeling.

Step 6: Turn Solutions Into Action

Now that you've explored your options, it's time to move.

Use ChatGPT to help you:

- Break the solution into steps
- Create a timeline
- Identify resources or support needed
- Build in accountability or measurement

Try:

> *"Help me turn this into a 3-step plan I can start this week."*
>
> *"What should I do first to get early feedback or traction?"*
>
> *"What would this look like if I mapped it over 30 days?"*
>
> *"Turn this into a checklist I can follow."*

Example:

You've decided to improve team communication using async updates.

Prompt:

> *"Build a simple rollout plan to test async check-ins for one week."*

ChatGPT might suggest:

1. Set expectations via a kickoff email
2. Choose a tool (Loom, Notion, Slack threads)
3. Pilot the check-ins with a 3-person team
4. Review feedback on Friday
5. Adjust or scale based on what you learn

Now you're moving forward—with structure, not stress.

The Problem Solver Protocol Prompt

Here's your full-process shortcut prompt:

> *"Help me work through this problem using a structured thinking process. I'll describe the situation, and you help me:*

1. Clarify the problem
2. Identify root causes
3. Reframe the challenge
4. Brainstorm solutions
5. Evaluate trade-offs
6. Create an action plan."

Paste in your situation and let ChatGPT walk you through step-by-step.

You've just turned chaos into clarity—in real time.

Bonus: Role-Based Problem Solving

Sometimes the fastest way to insight is to **switch perspectives**.

Prompt:

- "How would a therapist help me understand this?"
- "What would a startup advisor say about this bottleneck?"
- "What advice would a world-class designer give about improving this flow?"
- "If I were mentoring someone else with this exact problem, what would I tell them?"

ChatGPT can role-play any of these—and mirror back your wisdom in a new voice.

Recap: Solving Problems with Purpose

Let's recap the **Problem Solver Protocol**:

1. **Define the problem clearly**
2. **Separate symptoms from root causes**
3. **Reframe the challenge**
4. **Generate multiple solutions**
5. **Evaluate trade-offs**
6. **Create a clear, actionable plan**

With ChatGPT, you never have to stay stuck. You have a patient, structured, unbiased thinking partner available 24/7.

Whether you're solving a technical issue, a team challenge, a business dilemma, or a creative snag, this protocol gives you clarity fast—and confidence to move forward.

In the next chapter, we'll look at how to **reverse engineer success** using ChatGPT. Instead of starting from scratch, you'll learn how to study what already works and model it—with integrity, speed, and originality.

Let's keep moving forward, one solved problem at a time.

13

Reverse Engineer Anything

You've heard the phrase "don't reinvent the wheel." That's not laziness—it's strategy.

If someone else has already figured out how to:

- write viral content
- grow a thriving business
- build a compelling product
- captivate an audience
- master a difficult skill

...then your job isn't to start from zero.

Your job is to **reverse engineer what works**, understand why it works, and adapt it to your unique purpose, voice, and audience.

That's what this chapter is about: using ChatGPT to **deconstruct brilliance**, learn from it, and apply the insights with confidence.

This isn't copying. It's pattern recognition. And it's one of the fastest ways to level up your creativity, strategy, and output—especially when guided by a tool that can analyze and synthesize at lightning speed.

In this chapter, you'll learn:

- What reverse engineering is (and what it isn't)
- How to study content, campaigns, ideas, or workflows that work
- How to ask ChatGPT for structure, patterns, and psychological drivers
- How to apply what you learn—without mimicking or losing your originality

What Is Reverse Engineering?

Reverse engineering means **breaking something successful into its key components**, so you can understand how it works—and rebuild something similar for your own goals.

Think of it like this:

- You read a blog post that resonates deeply.
- You don't just say, "Wow, great post."
- You say, "What structure did they use? Why did it keep my attention? How did they open it? What emotional levers did they pull?"

You're studying the **underlying system**, not just the surface.

And once you see the system, you can rebuild it—with your content, your product, your audience, your values.

That's where ChatGPT becomes invaluable.

What You Can Reverse Engineer

You can use this strategy for almost anything:

- **Emails** that get high open and click-through rates
- **YouTube videos** with strong retention
- **Courses** with high completion rates
- **Landing pages** that convert
- **Books** that build a cult following
- **Speeches** that go viral
- **Newsletters** that people actually read
- **Pricing pages** that drive signups
- **Business models** that scale quickly
- **Habit systems** that actually work

If it has structure, purpose, and a result—it can be dissected and studied.

How to Reverse Engineer with ChatGPT (Step-by-Step)

Let's break it into a system.

Step 1: Identify a Model of Success

Start by selecting a piece of content, product, or system that achieved something *you* want to achieve.
Examples:

- A blog post that ranks on page 1
- An email funnel that led you to buy
- A book you couldn't put down

- A service page that made you book a call
- A YouTube video that held your attention for 15 minutes straight

Grab the content, link, or excerpt—and move to the next step.

Step 2: Feed It to ChatGPT for Structural Analysis

Ask ChatGPT to break it down.

Try:

> *"Here's a piece of content I admire. Break it into sections and describe the purpose of each part."*
>
> *"What structure or framework is this using? Can you name or label it?"*
>
> *"What emotions or psychological principles are being triggered here?"*
>
> *"Why is this likely to perform well for the target audience?"*

Example:
Paste a successful blog post and ask:

> *"Why does this post work so well? Break it into an outline and explain what each part is doing."*

ChatGPT might reply:

- **Hook:** Opens with a bold, contrarian statement that challenges the reader's assumptions

- **Problem setup:** Names a relatable frustration and amplifies the cost of not solving it
- **Solution preview:** Teases the payoff and stakes the claim: "You'll learn how to fix this in 3 steps"
- **Step-by-step structure:** Builds trust and authority through practical advice
- **Call to action:** Clear next step—share, comment, download, or book a call

Now you've got a **replicable skeleton**—not to copy, but to use as a flexible mold.

Step 3: Identify the Levers

Levers are the subtle forces that make something *feel good* or *work well*—even if the user doesn't notice them.

Ask:

> *"What psychological triggers are embedded in this?"*
> *"What types of storytelling, pacing, or tone are being used?"*
> *"How is trust being built quickly?"*
> *"What's motivating the reader/viewer to keep going?"*

Examples of levers:

- Curiosity (open loops, cliffhangers)
- Authority (social proof, credentials)
- Empathy (shared struggle, personal story)
- Specificity (clear numbers, tangible outcomes)
- Urgency (deadlines, scarcity)

- Belonging (identity, tribe language)

Once you see which levers are in play, you can pull them intentionally in your own work.

Step 4: Rebuild Your Version

Now it's time to apply what you've learned.

You can ask ChatGPT to help:

- "Using the same structure, create an outline for a blog post about [your topic]."
- "Help me apply this framework to my product launch page."
- "Write a YouTube script for my channel using this pacing and tone."
- "What would this same strategy look like for [my niche/audience]?"

You're not stealing. You're **mapping success principles onto your message.**

This accelerates learning, testing, and creation.

Example: Reverse Engineering a Viral Email

Let's say you subscribe to an email list that sends killer weekly newsletters. One of them gets shared widely, and you want to understand why.

You paste the email into ChatGPT and say:

> *"Deconstruct this email. What's the structure, tone, emotional journey, and reason it works?"*

ChatGPT might return:

Structure:

1. Attention-grabbing subject line
2. Personal anecdote to build connection
3. Surprising insight that challenges the reader
4. Actionable advice framed as a takeaway
5. Signature sign-off and PS with CTA

Tone: Warm, candid, lightly self-deprecating, high empathy

Emotional levers: Curiosity, resonance, trust, motivation

Why it works:

- Uses a "story → insight → tip" flow
- Shows vulnerability to increase relatability
- Offers value in <3 minutes of reading
- Clear takeaway the reader can apply

Now you ask ChatGPT:

> *"Can you help me write a weekly email in this same style about [topic I teach]?"*

And it does. You revise and personalize it—but the hard part (structure, flow, tone) is already handled.

That's the magic of the method.

Bonus: Reverse Engineer from Public Examples

You don't need insider access to brilliant strategy. The internet is full of public examples you can analyze.

Try feeding ChatGPT:

- Book chapters from Amazon previews
- Sales pages or landing pages from high-performing brands
- Podcast episode summaries
- TED Talk transcripts
- Tweet threads with 10k+ likes
- Course outlines on learning platforms

Then use prompts like:

- "Why is this structure effective for teaching or selling?"
- "How could I apply this same strategy to [my thing]?"
- "Rewrite this concept using my voice and niche."
- "What's a simpler version of this I could test this week?"

You now have *free mentorship* from some of the best minds in the world—filtered through a tireless thinking partner.

Ethics Reminder: Model, Don't Mimic

Let's be clear: **reverse engineering is not plagiarism.**

You're studying structure, rhythm, pacing, principles—not lifting someone else's words or ideas.

Use what works. Honor originality. Build with integrity.

Let ChatGPT help you:

- Make it your own
- Speak in your voice
- Align it with your values
- Serve your specific audience

Reverse engineering isn't about shortcuts. It's about *strategic creativity with clear eyes and open data.*

Recap: Build Backward to Move Forward

Here's the 4-step reverse engineering process:

1. **Find something that works** (a blog post, page, email, funnel, idea)
2. **Analyze it with ChatGPT** for structure, tone, levers, and flow
3. **Ask why it works** (psychology, storytelling, trust, curiosity)
4. **Apply the structure** to your content, idea, product, or system

You're no longer guessing.

You're modeling brilliance, refining strategy, and building on strong foundations.

In the next chapter, we'll look at how to **build systems and workflows** with ChatGPT—so you can scale your thinking and output consistently over time.

Let's keep going.

14

Systems That Think for You

There's a moment in every creative or strategic journey when you realize:

You don't need more hacks.

You need systems.

Hacks are quick wins. But systems are what **build momentum**, **save energy**, and **create freedom**.

And the best part? You don't have to build them alone.

With ChatGPT, you can create **thinking systems** that work *with* you—daily, weekly, and across all areas of your work and life. Systems that:

- Organize your thoughts
- Clarify your goals
- Automate brainstorming
- Speed up planning
- Surface patterns you'd otherwise miss

These aren't rigid checklists or cold automation. These are **adaptive, evolving workflows**—fueled by a smart assistant who never gets tired.

In this chapter, you'll learn how to:

- Design reusable thinking systems with ChatGPT
- Create prompt templates that work across contexts
- Build weekly workflows that boost creativity and reduce decision fatigue
- Develop rituals that turn reflection into progress

Let's turn your best thinking into something repeatable.

What Is a Thinking System?

A thinking system is any repeatable process that helps you:

- Frame problems
- Generate ideas
- Prioritize actions
- Clarify meaning
- Make better decisions

The difference between a random idea and a systemized process is this:

> *With a system, you don't have to* think about how to think.
>
> *You just plug in the problem—and the process begins.*

That's where ChatGPT shines. It turns your brain's best methods into flexible, scalable templates that you can return to again and again.

Step 1: Identify Your High-Leverage Thinking Tasks

Start by asking:

> *What do I think about every week that takes time, energy, or decision-making effort?*

Make a short list. For example:

- Planning the week
- Brainstorming content
- Reviewing progress
- Prioritizing tasks
- Writing social media posts
- Setting intentions
- Evaluating projects
- Coming up with new offers or features

These are perfect opportunities to build a ChatGPT-powered system.

Now let's start designing.

Step 2: Build Reusable Prompt Templates

A thinking system often starts with a **repeatable prompt**.

These are not one-time questions. They're frameworks you return to again and again—like digital rituals.

Here are examples you can adapt:

Weekly Planning Prompt

> *"It's Sunday night and I'm preparing for the week ahead. Help me:*

1. Identify my top 3 priorities
2. Break them into actionable tasks
3. Schedule focused work blocks
4. Spot potential distractions
5. Set a simple intention for how I want to feel this week"

Decision-Making Filter

> *"I'm trying to decide between [Option A] and [Option B]. Help me evaluate them based on:*

- Alignment with long-term goals
- Ease of implementation
- Energy cost
- Potential upside
- Gut instinct score (1–10)"

Content Creation Kickstart

> *"Each week I write content for my audience of [describe them]. Based on my current themes of [list], give me:*

- 5 content hooks
- 3 headline formulas
- A 3-post series idea
- One analogy that makes a complex idea simple"

Reflection and Reset

> *"Help me reflect on this past week by answering:*

1. What worked well?
2. What felt heavy or draining?
3. What am I proud of?
4. What needs to change next week?
5. What do I want more of?"

Project Planning System

> *"I have a new project: [describe it]. Help me break it down into:*

- Milestones
- Tasks
- Dependencies
- Deadlines
- Risks
- Resources I might need"

Save your favorite templates. Name them. Copy and paste them into your notes app or task manager. Return to them regularly.

This is how your brain gets faster: not by thinking harder, but by **removing friction**.

Step 3: Turn Templates into Weekly Workflows

Now let's make it real. Choose 3–5 thinking systems you want to use regularly. Assign them to different days or routines.

For example:

Day	Thinking System	Prompt Name
Monday	Weekly Planning	"Sunday Planning Ritual"
Wednesday	Content Ideation	"Midweek Creative Sprint"
Friday	Weekly Review & Reset	"Friday Reflection Flow"
Anytime	Project Planning	"Launch Prep Checklist"
On Demand	Decision-Making Support	"Clarity Filter Prompt"

You're not just using ChatGPT randomly. You're building a rhythm—a structure that supports your best thinking without starting from scratch.

Step 4: Layer in Modular Thinking Blocks

Modular blocks are mini-systems that you can mix, match, or combine for complex thinking.

For example:

SWOT Analysis Block

> *"Help me do a SWOT analysis (Strengths, Weaknesses, Opportunities, Threats) for [business/project idea]."*

Hook Generator Block

> *"Give me 10 content hooks using these formulas: curiosity, controversy, how-to, and personal story."*

Habit Troubleshooting Block

> *"I'm struggling to stay consistent with [habit]. Help me figure out why and suggest a 3-step fix."*

Use these modules to support deeper problem-solving or planning. They slot easily into your bigger systems.

Why Thinking Systems Save You Time

When you systemize your thinking with ChatGPT, you get:

- **Speed** – no more reinventing the wheel
- **Clarity** – structured prompts lead to structured thought
- **Focus** – you follow a clear track instead of chasing mental squirrels
- **Consistency** – your best thinking becomes repeatable
- **Freedom** – you free up brainpower for creation, not just management

Your system becomes your second brain. ChatGPT simply activates it on demand.

Advanced Move: Teach ChatGPT Your Systems

Once you've used a prompt template a few times, you can teach ChatGPT how *you* think.

Try:

> *"Act as my personal productivity assistant. I have a weekly system where I plan, review, and prioritize using the following steps. I'll paste them below. Once you understand them, help me execute this every Monday morning."*

Paste your process, and ChatGPT will remember it *within the conversation* and guide you accordingly.

This is the early stage of "prompt programming." You're teaching your AI to think like you do—and then helping it make you better.

Mini-Systems You Can Build Today

Need inspiration? Here are some small-but-mighty thinking systems you can create with ChatGPT:

- **Morning Intention Journal**
- → "Ask me 3 questions to center my focus and energy for the day."
- **Client Prep Routine**
- → "I have a call with a [type of client]. What questions should I ask? What value can I provide? What potential red flags should I look out for?"
- **Idea Tracker + Next Step**

- → "Here's an idea I had. Help me explore it in 3 ways, then suggest 1 simple test to try this week."
- **Content Repurposing Engine**
- → "Here's a blog post. Turn it into:
- 3 tweet threads
- 1 short video script
- 2 email tips
- 1 carousel summary"

Each system saves you time, energy, and decision fatigue. That's leverage.

Recap: Build Systems That Think for You

Let's review.

Thinking systems aren't complex automations. They're:

- Structured prompt templates
- Weekly workflows
- Modular mental tools
- Repeatable creative flows
- Personalized rituals

You now have the ability to:

- Organize your thinking
- Speed up decision-making
- Reduce overwhelm
- Scale your creativity

Most importantly, you're not just using ChatGPT to solve one-off problems—you're turning it into a **thinking partner that grows with you.**

In the next chapter, we'll dive into how to **think in frameworks** using ChatGPT—so you can simplify complexity, communicate ideas more clearly, and approach new challenges with confidence and clarity.

Let's keep building.

15

Think in Frameworks

If you've ever explained a big idea by drawing a box and two arrows, congratulations—you were thinking in a framework.

Frameworks are mental containers. They simplify the complex.

They reveal structure where others see chaos.

They help you clarify your own ideas—and communicate them clearly to others.

Whether you're planning a project, teaching a concept, solving a problem, or pitching an idea, frameworks save the day by:

- Making your thinking visible
- Creating repeatable logic
- Organizing messy inputs
- Allowing others to "see what you see"

The good news? You don't have to invent your own frameworks from scratch (though you can).

Many of the most powerful thinking tools in the world—like

SMART goals, Eisenhower matrix, the Hero's Journey—are just **well-labeled frameworks** anyone can use.

In this chapter, you'll learn how to:

- Use ChatGPT to discover and apply proven frameworks
- Build your own lightweight mental models
- Adapt frameworks to your unique goals and audience
- Turn complex thinking into clear visuals and step-by-step guidance

Let's begin.

What Is a Framework (and Why It Matters)?

A framework is a structured way of organizing information, decisions, or ideas.

Think of it like scaffolding. It doesn't give you all the answers—but it gives you **a place to put them.**

For example:

- A to-do list is not a framework.
- Eisenhower's urgent/important matrix *is*.
- A motivational quote is not a framework.
- The "Golden Circle" (Why → How → What) from Simon Sinek *is*.

Frameworks help you:

- Make better decisions
- Communicate more persuasively
- Break big ideas into digestible parts

- Reduce cognitive load
- See what's missing

And best of all?

> *You can use ChatGPT to access, remix, or create frameworks on demand.*

Step 1: Use Existing Frameworks to Speed Up Thinking

One of the fastest ways to improve your thinking is to **borrow models that already work.**

Let's say you're launching a product. You ask:

> *"What are some useful business frameworks I can use to plan a product launch?"*

ChatGPT might return:

- **AIDA**: Attention → Interest → Desire → Action (for marketing funnels)
- **SWOT**: Strengths, Weaknesses, Opportunities, Threats (for situational analysis)
- **4 Ps**: Product, Price, Place, Promotion (for positioning)
- **Lean Canvas**: One-page business model (for startup validation)

Instead of reinventing the wheel, you just plug your ideas into a format that sharpens them.

You can also ask:

> *"What frameworks do successful educators use to design effective lessons?"*
>
> *"What mental models help with making better life decisions?"*
>
> *"What productivity frameworks do top performers use to prioritize their week?"*

The key is this: **you're not starting from a blank page.** You're standing on proven structures and adapting them to your needs.

Step 2: Create Custom Frameworks with ChatGPT

Let's say you've developed your own process or idea, but it feels messy or abstract.

You can use ChatGPT to help structure it into a clean, repeatable framework.

Try:

> *"I teach people how to write nonfiction books. My process includes [list your steps]. Help me organize this into a memorable 3–5 part framework with simple labels."*

ChatGPT might return:

- **The WRITE Method**
- **W** – Work backward from your reader
- **R** – Refine your big idea
- **I** – Identify your structure
- **T** – Tackle the first draft
- **E** – Edit with empathy

Or:

> *"Turn my messy process into a step-by-step system with clear names and logic."*

You can even add constraints:

> *"Make it sound simple and modern."*
> *"Use a metaphor or acronym."*
> *"Keep it under 5 steps."*

You're creating your own **signature thought structure**—with AI as your co-architect.

Step 3: Use Frameworks to Solve Real Problems

Frameworks aren't just theoretical. They're powerful tools for decision-making, problem-solving, and ideation.

Let's say you're facing burnout. You ask ChatGPT:

> *"What frameworks can I use to understand or reduce burnout?"*

It might offer:

- **Maslow's Hierarchy of Needs** (Are your basic needs being met?)
- **The Energy Audit** (What gives vs. drains energy across physical, emotional, mental, spiritual domains?)
- **Job Demands-Resources Model** (Are your responsibilities growing faster than your resources?)

- **The 80/20 Rule** (Are you spending 80% of energy on 20% of results?)

Now you're not just feeling overwhelmed—you're looking at your life through structured lenses that lead to insight.

You can also use this method to:

- Break down a team conflict
- Diagnose a product problem
- Understand customer behavior
- Clarify a strategic choice
- Map out a habit change

When in doubt, ask:

> *"What frameworks would help me think through [insert your situation]?"*

Step 4: Translate Frameworks Into Visuals or Models

The power of a framework increases when you make it **visual**.

Why?

Because visuals allow people to "see" structure—especially helpful for communicating or teaching your ideas.

ChatGPT can't draw diagrams directly, but it can **describe visuals in detail**.

Try:

> *"Turn this 3-step framework into a diagram I can sketch on a whiteboard."*
>
> *"Describe what this model would look like visually using arrows, boxes, or shapes."*
>
> *"Suggest a metaphor I could use to represent this framework in a presentation."*

Example Prompt:

> *"I created a framework called The Clarity Triangle: Vision, Priorities, Execution. Help me visualize it as a simple diagram and suggest a story or metaphor to explain it."*

ChatGPT might return:

- A triangle with each side labeled
- Arrows pointing inward to "Alignment"
- A metaphor: "It's like calibrating a compass before a journey—you need all three points to find your true north."

Now you've got something **memorable and shareable.**

Step 5: Teach, Coach, and Lead Using Frameworks

One of the most powerful uses of frameworks is **teaching others how to think.**

With ChatGPT, you can create frameworks for:

- Onboarding a new hire
- Coaching a client
- Teaching a course
- Writing a book
- Pitching an idea
- Simplifying a complex insight

Try:

> *"I want to teach my audience how to build confidence. Help me create a 4-part framework that's easy to remember, actionable, and emotionally engaging."*

Or:

> *"Give me a coaching framework I can use with clients who feel stuck in indecision."*

Frameworks make your work **more impactful** because they give people language and structure they can *reuse.*

That's thought leadership.

Pitfall: Don't Over-Framework Everything

Not every idea needs a framework. If you try to squeeze every thought into a 4-box matrix, you'll end up reducing nuance where it's needed.

Use frameworks to **clarify**, not to flatten.

Ask:

- "Is this actually helpful, or just clever labeling?"

- "Does this framework simplify a real complexity—or over-simplify it?"
- "Will this help someone take action—or just sound smart?"

Remember, the best frameworks don't show off—they serve. Keep it human. Keep it helpful.

Recap: Frameworks That Multiply Your Thinking

Let's bring it all together.

Frameworks are:

- Mental structures that simplify complexity
- Tools for decision-making, communication, and teaching
- Accelerators for strategic and creative thinking

With ChatGPT, you can:

- Use existing frameworks to make better decisions
- Create custom frameworks to share your process
- Apply frameworks to real-world problems
- Turn frameworks into visuals and metaphors
- Teach others using simple, memorable systems

You're not just using AI to "get answers." You're building structured thinking tools that let you move faster, teach better, and lead with clarity.

In the next chapter, we'll turn to something a little more personal—**how to use ChatGPT to supercharge your personal growth, build self-awareness, and uncover blind spots** in your thinking and behavior.

Let's keep growing.

16

Reflect, Grow, Repeat

There's a hidden superpower inside ChatGPT—one that has nothing to do with writing emails, building business plans, or generating headlines.

It's this:

ChatGPT can help you become more self-aware.

Most people think of AI as a productivity booster. But the real transformation happens when you start using it as a **mirror**—a safe, objective, always-available reflection tool that helps you:

- Clarify your thoughts
- Notice your patterns
- Reframe your self-talk
- Spot blind spots
- Grow on purpose

In this chapter, you'll learn how to use ChatGPT as a **compassionate thinking partner** in your personal development journey—without cheesy affirmations, therapy-speak, or performative journaling.

This is about real growth. The kind that happens when insight leads to action.

Why Self-Reflection Is a Thinking Shortcut

Most people associate self-reflection with slowing down. In a way, that's true. But here's the paradox:

> *Slowing down your thoughts helps you speed up your progress.*

When you pause to ask better questions, revisit what worked (and what didn't), and look at your beliefs through a clear lens, you make sharper decisions faster. You stop repeating the same emotional loops. You start showing up with more clarity and intention.

Self-reflection isn't fluff. It's strategy.

And now you have a tool that never gets tired of asking "Why?"

Step 1: Use Guided Prompts for Weekly Reflection

One of the simplest ways to start a growth practice with ChatGPT is to create a **weekly reflection ritual.**

You don't have to stare at a blank journal. Just use a structured prompt like this:

> *"Act as my weekly reflection coach. Ask me five powerful questions about this past week that will help me grow,*

learn, and reset."

ChatGPT might respond with:

1. What was your proudest moment this week—and why did it matter to you?
2. What drained your energy most? What did you learn from that experience?
3. What moment brought unexpected joy or peace?
4. Where did you feel resistance, and what might that be telling you?
5. What's one thing you'd like to do differently next week?

You can answer directly in the chat, or just use the questions in your journal. Either way, you're engaging your **meta-cognition**—the process of thinking about your thinking.

That's where growth lives.

Step 2: Spot Patterns and Beliefs Holding You Back

Once you start capturing reflections, ChatGPT becomes even more useful—not just in prompting your thoughts, but in **analyzing them**.

Try:

> *"Here are my reflections from the past 3 weeks. What patterns do you notice in what I'm struggling with or focusing on?"*

Or:

> *"Based on what I've written, what beliefs or assumptions might be influencing my decisions?"*

ChatGPT isn't perfect—but it's surprisingly good at mirroring back themes and narratives you may not notice.

For example, it might say:

> *"You frequently mention fear of disappointing others. This could point to a people-pleasing tendency that's affecting how you set boundaries or prioritize your goals."*

Or:

> *"There's a recurring pattern of undervaluing your accomplishments, even when you achieve meaningful wins."*

This kind of gentle insight can spark real change—without judgment or shame.

Step 3: Reframe Limiting Thoughts in Real Time

We all have moments when our thoughts turn against us:

- "I'm behind."
- "I'm not good at this."
- "This always happens to me."
- "Why even try?"

These are cognitive distortions—flawed patterns of thinking that sound true but aren't.

The next time this happens, try this prompt:

> *"Help me reframe this limiting belief: [insert your thought]. Offer me a healthier perspective grounded in truth and possibility."*

Example:

You say: "I failed that presentation. I'm terrible at public speaking."

ChatGPT might respond:

> *"It's understandable to feel discouraged, but one moment doesn't define your skill. Every speaker has off days. What if this was a valuable learning experience, not a verdict on your ability? Let's identify what went wrong, what you did well, and how to grow from it."*

It doesn't invalidate your feelings. It helps you **move through them.**

Over time, this practice rewires how you think about setbacks, effort, and worth.

Step 4: Explore Identity and Purpose with Structured Prompts

Sometimes the hardest questions are the ones that matter most:

- Who am I becoming?
- What do I want more of in my life?
- Where am I settling out of fear?
- What would I do if I trusted myself fully?

You can ask ChatGPT to guide you through deeper inquiry:

> *"Ask me 10 meaningful questions to help me explore my identity, values, and direction in life."*

Or:

> *"Act like a personal development coach. Help me clarify my purpose by asking layered questions and giving me space to reflect."*

Example:

> *"What brings you alive—where you lose track of time, feel most useful, and come home to yourself? When was the last time you felt that?"*

You can use this process to write a life vision, articulate a mission, or even course-correct when you feel off track.

Step 5: Build a Self-Discovery System

Instead of reflecting only when you're overwhelmed, you can build a **self-discovery system** that helps you reflect regularly—without burnout.

Create a ChatGPT prompt like this:

> *"Every Friday, guide me through a 15-minute check-in. Ask about my highlights, lessons, emotions, relationships, and growth edge. Keep it structured and kind. At the end, suggest a focus word or intention for the week ahead."*

You now have a **repeatable ritual**. One that's private, nonjudgmental, and completely personalized.

You can also customize your system based on specific goals:

- Emotional regulation
- Confidence building
- Career clarity
- Leadership growth
- Relationship awareness

ChatGPT can help you track growth like a mirror—and a mentor.

Bonus: Process Emotions Without Spiraling

We've all been there: something triggers us, and our thoughts spiral.

Instead of venting to a friend (or bottling it up), try this:

> *"Act like a calm, nonjudgmental listener. I'm going to tell you what I'm feeling, and I want you to help me reflect and process it—without fixing or minimizing it."*

Then just type what's on your mind.

ChatGPT might respond:

> *"Thank you for sharing that. It makes sense you'd feel that way given the situation. Would you like help naming the emotion more precisely, or just space to explore what it means for you?"*

The goal isn't to get advice. It's to process. To feel heard. To reconnect with your wiser self.

You're giving yourself the gift of **emotional clarity**—in real time.

Caveats and Care

While ChatGPT can be a powerful tool for personal growth, it's not a therapist. It can't diagnose mental health issues, replace trauma-informed support, or navigate deeply personal dynamics.

But it can:

- Support reflection
- Ask better questions
- Offer perspective
- Reinforce your values
- Help you learn from your life

Always pair AI with discernment—and real human support when needed.

Recap: Use AI to Grow from the Inside Out

You don't need to wait for a breakdown or burnout to grow.

You can build awareness *now*—through regular reflection, inquiry, and intention.

Here's how to use ChatGPT as a personal growth partner:

1. Use weekly reflection prompts to clarify lessons and patterns
2. Analyze recurring thoughts to spot limiting beliefs
3. Reframe negative self-talk into constructive truth

4. Explore identity and purpose with guided inquiry
5. Build a ritualized system for tracking emotional and mind-set growth

You're not just thinking faster now.

You're thinking deeper—and wiser.

In the next chapter, we'll explore how to **use ChatGPT to learn anything faster**—turning AI into your personal tutor, curriculum builder, and explainer-in-chief.

Let's keep going.

17

Learn Anything Faster

There's a popular myth about learning—that it takes years of painstaking repetition, textbooks, and expensive courses to get good at something.

But in the age of AI, a new truth is emerging:

> ***You don't need to know everything. You need to know how to learn anything—fast.***

Whether you want to:

- Understand a new industry
- Master a skill
- Prepare for a certification
- Pick up a new language
- Brush up on technical concepts
- Or just "get smart" on a topic you've never explored before...

ChatGPT can serve as your **on-demand tutor, explainer, quiz**

generator, and learning strategist—adapting to your style, speed, and goals.

In this chapter, you'll learn how to:

- Turn ChatGPT into a flexible, personalized teacher
- Break complex topics into bite-sized lessons
- Ask better questions that speed up understanding
- Build a self-guided curriculum for any subject
- Use AI to test your knowledge and boost retention

Let's unlock your learning engine.

Why Speed Learning Matters More Than Ever

In a world where industries evolve overnight, information doubles every few months, and tools get outdated in weeks—not years—the ability to **rapidly upskill** is no longer a nice-to-have.

It's survival.

But the traditional education system wasn't built for speed. It was built for standardization.

ChatGPT flips the model. It allows you to:

- Skip to what matters
- Learn in your preferred format (bullets, analogies, Q&A, etc.)
- Review anything, anytime, without waiting for a course
- Learn in *context*—based on your job, goals, or interests

This isn't about shortcuts. It's about **efficient, self-directed learning**, tailored to you.

Step 1: Turn ChatGPT Into a Personal Tutor

The simplest place to start? Just say:

> *"Act as my personal tutor. I want to learn [topic]. Break it into logical sections and teach me the basics in a way that's easy to understand—even if I'm a beginner."*

For example:

- "Teach me the basics of stock market investing."
- "Explain neural networks in plain English, as if I'm 12 years old."
- "Help me understand the U.S. Constitution, one concept at a time."

ChatGPT can tailor its tone, format, and depth to your level. You can ask for:

- Definitions
- Analogies
- Examples
- Diagrams (described)
- Real-world applications
- Interactive questions

You're not reading a dry textbook. You're having a **conversation with an intelligent guide.**

Step 2: Build a Custom Learning Path

Let's say you want to master a new topic over the next 30 days—copywriting, public speaking, climate science, real estate, you name it.

Try this prompt:

> *"Help me build a 4-week self-paced learning curriculum to understand [topic]. Include weekly goals, recommended resources (free if possible), and specific practice activities."*

ChatGPT might respond with:

Week 1: Foundations

- Learn core terms and basic concepts
- Read [introductory resource]
- Watch [video series or TED Talk]
- Daily activity: summarize one key idea in your own words

Week 2: Apply and Explore

- Dive into subtopics
- Create a mind map
- Try mini-projects or mock scenarios
- Reflect: what confuses or excites you?

...and so on.

You now have a roadmap—*your own personal syllabus.* And it adapts every time you ask a new question.

Step 3: Break Complex Ideas into Understandable Chunks

Sometimes you don't need a whole curriculum—you just need to *get* something that feels complicated.

Try this:

> *"Explain [topic] in simple terms, like you're teaching someone with no background."*
>
> *"Now explain it again using a metaphor I'd understand as a [writer/teacher/parent/designer/etc.]."*
>
> *"Give me the 80/20 version—the most important 20% of ideas I need to know."*
>
> *"Summarize this article in 5 bullet points and tell me what matters most."*

This isn't cheating. This is **accelerated clarity**.

When something clicks faster, you retain it longer—and use it sooner.

Step 4: Learn by Teaching (With ChatGPT's Help)

Want to *really* understand something? Teach it.

ChatGPT can simulate that process for you. For example:

> *"I just learned about [topic]. Ask me 5 questions to test my understanding."*
>
> *"Pretend I'm your student. I want to teach you what I've learned. Ask clarifying questions and correct me if I get anything wrong."*
>
> *"Help me explain [concept] to a 10-year-old. Rewrite what I said to make it clearer."*

You're now **applying the Feynman Technique**—one of the fastest ways to retain and clarify knowledge.

It works like this:

1. Learn the concept
2. Try to teach it simply
3. Find where your explanation breaks
4. Refine and simplify again

ChatGPT makes this fast, frictionless, and fun.

Step 5: Generate Flashcards, Quizzes, and Practice Prompts

Studying for a test? Prepping for a certification? Just want to remember what you've read?

Use ChatGPT to build your own memory tools.

Try:

> *"Make me 20 flashcards on the fundamentals of [topic]. Use a Q&A format."*
>
> *"Create a quiz to test my knowledge of [subject]. Include answers and explanations."*
>
> *"Turn this article into 10 multiple choice questions to help me review."*
>
> *"Give me a scenario-based challenge to apply what I've learned."*

The result? You move from **passive absorption** to **active engagement**—the key to deeper learning.

Bonus: Learn on the Go with Bite-Sized Prompts

Want to turn downtime into learning time?

Save mobile-friendly prompts like these:

- "Give me a 1-minute explanation of [topic] each morning this week."
- "Send me a daily micro-lesson on [subject]. Keep it under 5 bullets."
- "Ask me one question a day to build my knowledge of [topic]."

You can paste these into your notes app or texting platform. Now learning fits into your real life—not the other way around.

Case Study: 7 Days to Understand the Stock Market

Let's walk through an example.

Say you're a complete beginner who wants to grasp the basics of investing.

Start with:

> *"Act as my 7-day crash course tutor. Help me understand the stock market by breaking it into daily lessons, each under 500 words."*

ChatGPT returns:

- **Day 1**: What is the stock market and how does it work?
- **Day 2**: Stocks, ETFs, mutual funds—what's the difference?
- **Day 3**: Risk vs. return, diversification, and time horizons

- **Day 4**: How to read a stock chart or ticker
- **Day 5**: What influences stock prices (news, earnings, sentiment)
- **Day 6**: Long-term investing vs. day trading
- **Day 7**: How to open a brokerage account and get started safely

You now have a **digestible, accelerated learning plan**—no YouTube rabbit holes required.

Caution: Don't Skip Real-World Application

Learning is not just input—it's output.

ChatGPT helps you understand faster. But real mastery comes when you **do something with what you've learned.**

That could mean:

- Writing a short article
- Giving a mini-presentation
- Launching a small project
- Teaching someone else
- Making a real-world decision

Always ask:

> *"How can I use this knowledge today?"*

Then ask ChatGPT:

> *"Suggest 3 small ways to apply this concept this week."*
> *"What's one mini-project I can do in the next 24 hours*

to practice this skill?"

Knowledge is power—but only when it's in motion.

Recap: Learn Anything Faster with AI

ChatGPT isn't just a productivity tool. It's your **accelerated learning assistant**—always available, always adaptable.

Here's what to do:

1. Use it as a **personal tutor** to explain anything in simple terms
2. Build a **learning path** or curriculum tailored to your goals
3. Break down complex ideas into easy-to-grasp chunks
4. Test your understanding by **teaching back**
5. Reinforce your memory with **flashcards and quizzes**
6. Apply what you learn through real-world action
7. Repeat as needed—learning is never one-and-done

You already have curiosity. You already have the desire to grow.

Now you have a tool to match your pace.

In the next chapter, we'll zoom out and explore how to **scale your creativity and impact using AI as a multiplier**—so you can stop working harder and start working smarter.

Let's go bigger.

18

Multiply Your Output

Let's face it: some days it feels like your brain is full... and yet, your to-do list is still hungry.

You sit down to write, and the words don't flow.

You try to finish a project, and another one pops up.

You solve one problem... and two more show up in your inbox.

Here's the truth:

> *Most of us don't have a productivity problem.*
> *We have a **mental bandwidth problem**.*

The secret isn't working harder—it's learning how to **multiply your output without multiplying your stress**.

This is where ChatGPT becomes a true force multiplier. It helps you:

- Start faster
- Finish quicker
- Organize better
- Repurpose more

- Deliver higher-quality work—at scale

In this chapter, we'll explore:

- How to set up "content factories" with ChatGPT
- How to go from one idea to ten deliverables
- How to use AI for project management, writing, planning, and execution
- How to build momentum using creative batching
- Why multiplying output doesn't mean diluting quality

Let's turn your best ideas into a steady stream of high-leverage results.

Why Output Is the New Competitive Advantage

You've probably heard the phrase "done is better than perfect."

But in the age of AI, there's a new mantra emerging:

> ***"Done well, done fast, and done often wins."***

The ability to consistently create, deliver, and iterate on your ideas—without sacrificing clarity or creativity—is the new edge in every industry.

ChatGPT isn't just about speeding up individual tasks. It's about building an **output engine** that helps you:

- Write more content
- Launch more projects
- Test more offers
- Communicate more clearly

- Execute more consistently

And it all starts with how you think about your work.

Step 1: Build Repeatable Output Templates

The first step in multiplying output is removing friction at the start of a task.

That's where **prompt templates** come in.

Let's say you regularly create:

- Blog posts
- Newsletters
- Social media threads
- Marketing emails
- Meeting agendas
- Workshop outlines
- Project plans

Instead of writing from scratch, create prompt templates like:

> *"Act as my copywriting assistant. Write a blog post outline based on this idea: [insert idea]. Use a hook, subheadings, and a strong call to action."*
>
> *"Turn this blog post into a 5-post Instagram carousel. Each slide should have one key point, written in a friendly, helpful tone."*
>
> *"Create a launch email sequence for this offer: [insert description]. Include subject lines and preview text."*

The key? You create **once**, then output in **multiple directions**.

Step 2: Repurpose Like a Pro

Every piece of content or thinking you create can be turned into *at least* five others.

Try this with ChatGPT:

> *"I wrote this blog post. Help me turn it into:*
>
> 1. A 3-part email series
> 2. A short YouTube script
> 3. A LinkedIn post with an engaging question
> 4. A checklist version
> 5. A podcast interview outline based on the same ideas"

Or:

> *"I gave a talk on this topic. Help me break it into 10 tweets, each one punchy and valuable."*

Suddenly, one idea becomes ten assets—without ten times the effort.

This is how thought leaders operate. It's not about endless new ideas.

It's about **leveraging one great idea across many formats.**

Step 3: Use Batching to Stay in Flow

Task-switching kills momentum. So instead of bouncing between content, emails, meetings, and planning—**batch your tasks with ChatGPT as your co-creator.**

Examples:

- **Batch writing**: Create 3 blog post drafts in one sitting using structured prompts.
- **Batch ideation**: Ask for 25 content ideas in one session, then sort and schedule them later.
- **Batch planning**: Design your next 6 weeks of content, launches, or videos in one go.

ChatGPT makes batching easier because it *thinks with you.*

You're not generating from scratch—you're shaping output in a flow state.

Step 4: Build Output Systems for Projects and Teams

If you're juggling multiple deliverables, projects, or collaborators, ChatGPT can help you organize your thinking—and your systems.

Try:

> *"Help me map out the steps for launching a new podcast. Include planning, scripting, promotion, and scheduling."*

Or:

> *"Create a project plan with milestones and deadlines for publishing a digital product in 4 weeks."*

You can even ask:

> *"What tasks should I delegate vs. automate vs. do myself on this project?"*

Now ChatGPT becomes your **execution partner**, not just an idea generator.

And if you lead a team?

You can design reusable templates for:

- Onboarding new team members
- Planning meetings
- Writing briefs
- Reviewing content
- Creating SOPs (standard operating procedures)

Step 5: Scale Quality Without Losing Your Voice

Many people worry that more output means watered-down work.

It doesn't have to.

When you use ChatGPT to **amplify your voice**, not replace it, you can:

- Maintain quality
- Protect your standards
- Enhance your clarity
- Improve with each iteration

Try this:

> *"Here's a rough draft I wrote. Help me punch it up without losing my tone. Make it more concise, clear, and engaging."*

Or:

> *"Act as an editor. Give me feedback on clarity, structure, and flow—but don't rewrite everything. Just help me level up my original."*

You're not outsourcing your thinking. You're **amplifying your execution**.

Mini-Output Engines You Can Build Today

Here are some "output engines" you can set up using ChatGPT—ready to go whenever you are:

Content Engine

> *"Each week, help me generate 3 content ideas, 1 blog post draft, 1 newsletter, and 5 social media posts based on my themes of [insert themes]."*

Promotion Engine

> *"For every product I launch, generate a:*

- 5-email sequence
- Social post calendar
- Product description
- FAQ doc"

Speaking Engine

"When I have a podcast or talk coming up, help me:

- Draft talking points
- Write a short bio
- Create a slide outline
- Prepare for Q&A"

Client Delivery Engine

"For each client, help me:

- Draft the proposal
- Create a kickoff agenda
- Outline the project
- Write the wrap-up summary"

You don't just have systems.
You have **repeatable results**.

Recap: Multiply Output Without Burning Out

You don't need more hours in the day.
You need a better way to **convert ideas into results.**
With ChatGPT, you can:

1. Use prompt templates to start faster
2. Repurpose everything into multiple formats
3. Batch content, ideas, or planning sessions
4. Build execution systems for projects and teams

5. Maintain quality while increasing consistency and scale

Your ideas deserve more than one life.

Now, they can have ten.

In the next chapter, we'll look at the **future of thinking**—and how to design a personal "second brain" using AI to remember, reflect, and evolve alongside you.

Let's go even deeper.

19

Build Your Second Brain

What do you do with your best ideas?

The ones that hit you in the shower.

The ones you scribbled in a notebook months ago.

The ones you half-remember, but can't find when you need them.

If you're like most people, your best thinking ends up scattered across sticky notes, apps, browser tabs, and random text messages to yourself.

But what if you had a system that remembered **everything**—and helped you connect, refine, and reuse your thoughts?

Welcome to the concept of the **second brain**—a term popularized by Tiago Forte to describe a digital system that extends your memory, organizes your thinking, and gives you instant access to your past ideas and knowledge.

> *Now, with ChatGPT, building that second brain has never been easier—or more powerful.*

In this chapter, you'll learn how to:

- Create a second brain using AI and simple tools
- Use ChatGPT to organize, tag, and summarize your thoughts
- Turn scattered notes into searchable knowledge
- Link ideas across time to improve insight and creativity
- Set up your second brain for creative output and decision-making

This isn't just about note-taking. It's about **thinking better—over time.**

What Is a Second Brain (And Why You Need One)?

Your first brain—your biological one—is amazing. It's capable of intuition, creativity, emotion, and problem-solving.

But it's also limited:

- It forgets things
- It gets overwhelmed
- It doesn't organize information well
- It struggles to track everything across weeks, months, and years

Your **second brain** solves that.

It's a trusted, external system where you store your ideas, learnings, insights, and projects so that your mind is free to focus on the present—not constantly trying to recall the past.

A second brain gives you:

- Mental clarity
- Faster recall
- Creative connections
- A sense of intellectual momentum

With ChatGPT as your assistant, it becomes not just a storage tool—but a **thinking partner.**

Step 1: Choose Your Second Brain Tool

You don't need a fancy app to build your second brain.
You can use:

- Notion
- Evernote
- Obsidian
- Google Docs
- Apple Notes
- Logseq
- Roam Research
- Or even a simple folder system on your computer

What matters is that it's:

- Searchable
- Flexible
- Easy to access
- Consistent

ChatGPT doesn't store your notes for you, but it can **help you organize, structure, summarize, and recall** what you've stored elsewhere.

Step 2: Capture Notes and Ideas with Context

Most people take disjointed notes. A quote here. A sentence there. No tags. No context.

Your second brain thrives on **rich, searchable context**.

Next time you capture something—an article summary, a book note, a personal insight—ask ChatGPT to help you format it.

Try:

> *"Summarize this article into 5 takeaways. Include a quote, a question it raises, and how I might apply it."*

Or:

> *"Here's a paragraph I wrote. Create metadata: what is this about, why does it matter, and where should I store it in my second brain?"*

ChatGPT can generate tags, titles, summaries, and cross-references.

It's like having a librarian follow you around, quietly making sure your thoughts are cataloged and ready to be rediscovered.

Step 3: Organize Using PARA or Similar Frameworks

Tiago Forte's **PARA method** is a simple structure for organizing your digital life:

- **P**rojects: short-term efforts with outcomes
- **A**reas: ongoing responsibilities
- **R**esources: useful reference materials
- **A**rchives: inactive or completed items

You can use ChatGPT to sort content into these categories.

Try:

> *"Help me categorize these 20 notes into PARA buckets."*
>
> *"Suggest which of my notes are Projects vs. Resources."*
>
> *"Reformat this brainstorm so I can file it under a Resource topic."*

ChatGPT adds logic and language to your folders. It turns chaos into clarity.

Step 4: Link Ideas Across Time

One of the most powerful benefits of a second brain is **idea linking**—seeing patterns between concepts that might seem unrelated at first.

For example:

- A quote from a book aligns with a lesson from a podcast
- A journal entry connects with a business challenge
- A question you asked months ago now has an answer

You can prompt ChatGPT to surface these connections:

> *"I've saved notes on these topics: [list topics]. What patterns or themes do you see?"*

> *"Cross-reference these 3 notes and suggest a unifying insight."*
> *"Turn these ideas into a single framework or principle."*

Now your second brain becomes more than a storage unit.
It becomes a **thinking engine.**

Step 5: Use It to Fuel Output and Decision-Making

Once your ideas are organized and connected, you can use ChatGPT to turn them into action.
Try:

> *"Pull from my notes on productivity, habits, and flow states to help me write a blog post."*
> *"Based on these insights from past coaching sessions, what patterns can I bring into my next presentation?"*
> *"Summarize everything I've learned about negotiation into a 5-step checklist."*

This is how your second brain becomes an **output multiplier**. It turns stored knowledge into shareable, strategic content.

Bonus: Personal Reflection + Life Insights

Your second brain isn't just for work.
You can use it to track:

- Personal development
- Emotional insights
- Decisions you've made

- Patterns in your relationships
- Spiritual or philosophical reflections

ChatGPT can help you:

> *"Summarize my past 3 journal entries. What emotions and themes do you see?"*
> *"Help me tag and organize life lessons I've recorded over the past year."*
> *"Turn these notes into a personal values statement."*

This transforms your second brain from a tool... into a **mirror.**

Building Blocks of a Second Brain with ChatGPT

Here's a simple framework for using ChatGPT to build your second brain:

1. **Capture**

- Use voice, text, or highlights to collect thoughts
- Ask ChatGPT to format or summarize the input

1. **Organize**

- Apply PARA or another method with AI help
- Let ChatGPT auto-suggest categories or tags

1. **Link**

- Prompt AI to identify themes or connections

- Use ChatGPT to cluster ideas into frameworks

1. **Reflect**

- Ask questions about trends in your thoughts
- Review previous entries and gain insights

1. **Create**

- Turn your thinking into articles, talks, or action plans
- Use ChatGPT to draft, expand, or reframe content from your brain

Common Pitfalls (and How to Avoid Them)

Mistake 1: Capturing too much, using too little.
Solution: Set a weekly review. Ask ChatGPT,

> *"Summarize what I've saved this week and suggest one idea to revisit or act on."*

Mistake 2: Forgetting what you saved.
Solution: Create index pages or summaries. Prompt:

> *"Give me a dashboard-style summary of my top notes across categories."*

Mistake 3: Letting it get messy again.
Solution: Build a monthly cleanup ritual. Ask:

> *"Help me identify duplicate or outdated notes and clean*

up my second brain."

Recap: Your Second Brain = Long-Term Thinking Power

Your brain isn't failing you. It's just full.

A second brain gives you space to think clearly, act intentionally, and **build momentum over time**.

Here's how to create it with ChatGPT:

1. Use your favorite note tool (Notion, Obsidian, etc.)
2. Capture thoughts with context using ChatGPT
3. Organize using frameworks like PARA
4. Link ideas and extract deeper insights
5. Turn reflections into real-world output
6. Maintain it with light, regular rituals

This is how you think faster *and* smarter.

Not just today—but long-term.

In the final chapter, we'll explore how to stay ethically aligned in an AI-powered world—and how to use these tools without losing your humanity, voice, or values.

Let's finish strong.

20

Think Ethically, Use Wisely

By now, you've seen how ChatGPT can help you write faster, learn deeper, brainstorm better, and build thinking systems that work for you.

But here's the most important truth we'll leave you with:

> ***The tools don't define the thinker. The thinker defines the tools.***

We're entering an age where AI isn't just something in the background—it's a collaborator in the way we think, create, and communicate. That means we're no longer just users of technology.

We're **shapers** of it.

And that comes with a responsibility: to think **ethically**, use **wisely**, and never forget the human element behind every keystroke.

This final chapter will explore:

- Why ethical thinking matters in an AI-powered world

- The biggest risks (and how to avoid them)
- How to maintain your originality and voice
- The human strengths AI can't replace
- A code of conduct for smart, responsible AI use

Let's finish strong—and grounded.

The Ethics of AI: Why It Matters More Than Ever

ChatGPT isn't sentient. It doesn't have intent or consciousness. But *how we use it* reflects our choices, character, and clarity.

Ethics in AI use isn't just about right or wrong. It's about **respect**:

- Respect for your audience
- Respect for creators
- Respect for the truth
- Respect for your own integrity

As AI gets smarter, the temptation to over-rely on it—or use it deceptively—grows.

So does the potential for misinformation, laziness, and dehumanization.

But there's another path.

One where AI becomes a tool for **amplifying human values**, not replacing them.

5 Common Misuses of ChatGPT (And What to Do Instead)

Let's look at some traps—and how to rise above them.

1. Copy-Paste Creation Without Attribution

× Taking AI output and claiming it as entirely your own original work.

✓ Use ChatGPT as a *co-creator*, not a ghostwriter. Add your voice, edits, and insights. If you adapt or remix, consider giving credit.

2. Generating Harmful, Biased, or False Information

× Using AI to reinforce stereotypes, spread unverified claims, or game systems.

✓ Be a filter, not a funnel. Double-check facts. Avoid prompts that weaponize the model. Prioritize truth over speed.

3. Replacing Critical Thinking with Blind Trust

× Letting ChatGPT make decisions for you without evaluation.

✓ Always review. Ask follow-up questions. Compare multiple sources. AI is a spark, not a verdict.

4. Using AI to Manipulate, Not Inform

× Writing manipulative sales copy, fake reviews, or misleading narratives.

✓ Strive for clarity, honesty, and transparency. Good marketing informs and inspires—it doesn't deceive.

5. Neglecting Human Connection

✕ Automating everything until your work sounds robotic.

✓ Re-insert your warmth. Tell real stories. Speak from lived experience. Don't lose the **you** in your work.

How to Preserve Your Voice in an AI-World

The fastest way to sound like everyone else? Let ChatGPT do all the talking.

But the most powerful creators—marketers, writers, entrepreneurs, educators—stand out because their work is **personalized** and **human**.

Here's how to keep your voice sharp:

- Tweak tone and phrasing to sound like *you*
- Add stories from your life or work
- Use ChatGPT for scaffolding, then rewrite in your natural rhythm
- Create a "voice guide" and prompt ChatGPT to match it

> *"Here's how I write: concise, warm, a little witty, always practical. Rewrite this paragraph in that style."*

ChatGPT is amazing at mimicry—but *you* are the original.

What AI Can't Replace

AI is fast.

AI is versatile.

AI is impressive.

But AI is **not human**.

Here's what it can't replicate (and likely never will):

- Lived experience
- Moral judgment
- Empathy
- Intuition
- Imagination grounded in personal emotion
- The willingness to be vulnerable, messy, or imperfect

In other words: **your humanity is not a bug. It's the feature.**

The most compelling work you'll ever produce won't be perfect. It will be *real.*

A Personal Code of AI Conduct

Want to use AI responsibly and confidently? Start with a personal code.

Here's one to adapt or adopt:

1. **I use AI to assist, not replace, my thinking.**
2. **I give credit when I collaborate with AI, especially in public-facing work.**
3. **I verify facts before treating them as truth.**
4. **I avoid prompts that create harm, misinformation, or disrespect.**
5. **I refine AI outputs to reflect my ethics, voice, and intent.**
6. **I embrace curiosity and learn how to use the tool better each day.**
7. **I prioritize integrity over ease.**
8. **I remember: the tool is not the thinker. I am.**

When you approach AI from this foundation, you stay centered—even as the tech evolves.

The Future of Thinking: Human + Machine, Not Human vs. Machine

The question isn't "Will AI replace us?"

The question is:

> ***How will we show up as thinkers, creators, and leaders in an AI-augmented world?***

The most exciting future is a hybrid one—where human wisdom and machine efficiency combine to solve problems faster, express ideas more clearly, and unlock creativity that changes lives.

You've spent this book building that capacity:

- You know how to prompt better
- Think faster
- Capture and apply ideas
- Learn in weeks what used to take months
- Multiply output without burning out
- Reflect deeply—and ethically

You didn't just learn how to use ChatGPT.

You learned how to use your mind—more effectively, more intentionally, more powerfully.

Final Thought: The Tool Is Yours—Use It Well

So here you are.

Twenty chapters later, with a clearer mind, sharper tools, and a system that supports your speed, your growth, and your integrity.

Now what?

That's up to you.

You can:

- Launch a business faster
- Build a second brain
- Learn that thing you've always wanted to
- Write the book, start the podcast, fix the workflow
- Have better conversations—with others *and* yourself
- Or just feel more confident navigating the future

Whatever you do, just remember:

> *ChatGPT is not the source of your creativity.* You are.
>
> *It's not the end of thinking. It's a tool for better thinking.*
>
> *The future belongs to the humans who collaborate—wisely, ethically, and bravely—with machines.*

Now go think faster.

And go think well.

21

Conclusion: The Future Thinker Is You

In the pages you've just finished, we've explored more than just tools, tactics, or productivity tips.

We've mapped out a new way of thinking—one that's faster, smarter, more collaborative, and more intentional. A way of thinking that embraces AI as a partner, not a crutch. One that treats technology as a canvas, not a replacement for creativity.

Here's what you now know:

✓ You don't need to start from scratch. You can start with structure.

✓ You don't need to wait for the perfect idea. You can generate, refine, and iterate on demand.

✓ You don't need to fear AI. You can shape it with your voice, your vision, and your values.

You've learned how to:

- Use ChatGPT to clarify thoughts and generate new ones
- Prompt like a pro to get consistent, quality results
- Break through mental blocks and brainstorm without limits
- Build your own second brain and accelerate learning

- Multiply your creative output—without multiplying your stress
- Stay grounded in ethical, responsible, human-centered use

That's not just productivity. That's transformation.

What Happens Next Is Up to You

This isn't the end of the road. It's the beginning of a new way to navigate it.

Whether you're building a business, growing in your career, launching a creative project, or simply trying to keep up with the pace of modern life—you now have an edge.

You have a tool.

You have a system.

You have a mindset.

More importantly, you have **momentum**.

One Final Prompt

If you remember nothing else from this book, remember this:

> *You don't need to be the smartest person in the room. You just need to be the one who thinks with the most clarity, speed, and intention.*

And now you know how.

So the next time you face a blank page, a complex problem, or a wild idea...

Ask better questions.

Think out loud.

Use your tools.
Trust your voice.
And let your thoughts move—faster.

About the Author

James Douglas is a writer and researcher based in Nashville, Tennessee. He enjoys exploring topics like artificial intelligence, fitness, and personal growth, with a focus on making complex ideas practical and accessible. James also writes books fueled by personal passion, aiming to inspire and empower readers in every season of life.

www.ingramcontent.com/pod-product-compliance
Lightning Source LLC
LaVergne TN
LVHW052326200926
848481LV00002B/683
* 9 7 9 8 2 3 1 8 4 2 2 7 8 *